Other Books by Penny  S0-BYZ-123

Thanksgiving: The True Story

Adventurous Women:
Eight True Stories About Women Who Made a Difference

Rosie the Riveter:
Women Working on the Home Front in World War II

Where the Action Was:
Women War Correspondents in World War II

Girls:
A History of Growing Up Female in America

Corpses, Coffins, and Crypts:
A History of Burial

Madam C. J. Walker:
Building a Business Empire

Mother Jones and the March of the Mill Children

Fannie Lou Hamer and the Fight for the Vote

Women in Society:
United States of America

Breaking the Chains:
The Crusade of Dorothea Lynde Dix

Spies:
Women in the Civil War

Toilets, Bathtubs, Sinks and Sewers:
A History of the Bathroom

Strike! The Bitter Struggle of American Workers

A Woman Unafraid

The Achievements of
Frances Perkins

PENNY COLMAN

ASJA PRESS
NEW YORK   BLOOMINGTON

A Woman Unafraid: The Achievements of Frances Perkins

ASJA Press
an imprint of iUniverse, Inc.

iUniverse books may be ordered through booksellers or by contacting:

iUniverse
1663 Liberty Drive
Bloomington, IN 47403
www.iuniverse.com
1-800-Authors (1-800-288-4677)

Because of the dynamic nature of the Internet, any Web addresses or links contained in this book may have changed since publication and may no longer be valid.

ISBN: 978-1-4502-0773-7 (sc)

Printed in the United States of America

iUniverse rev. date: 2/3/2010

For K. C. Compton,
a wise, witty, and wonderful friend

Contents

Contents

Acknowledgments

Special thanks to Elaine D. Trehub, Mount Holyoke College Archives, South Hadley, Massachusetts, and to Judson Mac-Laury, Office of the Assistant Secretary for Policy, U.S. Department of Labor, for their enthusiastic and helpful assistance in providing materials and photographs. Also thanks to Gail Paris for her special involvement with this book. The following people also kindly provided assistance: Mary Gratton, National Women's Hall of Fame, Seneca Falls, New York; Paulette Manos, Martin P. Catherwood Library, Cornell University, Ithaca, New York; Jane Seigel-Rogers, Rare Book and Manuscript Library Columbia University, New York, New York; Peter Meyer Filardo, Tamiment Library, New York University, New York, New York; Polly Cutler, Worcester Historical Museum, Worcester, Massachusetts; Paul McLaughlin, Franklin D. Roosevelt Library, Hyde Park, New York; and the staff members of Tourist Information Centers in Newcastle and Damariscotta, Maine.

In addition, thank you to the following people for granting me permission to quote from various sources: Susanna W. Coggeshall, Frances Perkins's daughter; Kenneth A. Lohf, Librarian for Rare Books and Manuscripts; and Ronald J. Grele, Director Columbia University, Oral History Research, to quote from the Frances Perkins Papers, Rare Book and Manuscript Library, Columbia University, and Frances Perkins Oral History, Colum-

ix

bia University Oral History Research, Columbia University, New York, New York; and Anne C. Edmonds, Librarian, Mount Holyoke College, South Hadley, Massachusetts, to quote from Frances Perkins's letters.

As always, I am grateful to my three sons Jonathan, David, and Stephen for their lively discussions, thoughtful insights, terrific music, and love. I am also grateful to Linda Hickson for her encouragement and for reading each and every draft of this manuscript.

A Woman Unafraid

CHAPTER ONE

Cockroaches
and a Tricorn Hat

1880–1898

"I could talk well...."

Her first day at work as secretary of labor of the United States, Frances Perkins pulled out the drawers of her desk and found cockroaches. It wasn't the first time Frances Perkins had seen cockroaches. As a social worker, she saw cockroaches all the time when she visited the dingy, dreary apartments where poor people lived. But now she was head of the Department of Labor in Washington, D.C., and a member of the president's cabinet, the first woman cabinet member in American history.

It was a terrible time in America. Ever since the stock market crash on October 24, 1929, the economy had gotten worse and worse. Businesses closed down. Millions of people lost their jobs. They ran out of money and couldn't pay for a place to live or food to eat. If they were lucky, they had a tent, or found an abandoned shack, or a cardboard box, or built something out of scraps of wood or metal sheets. They stood in long lines to get free food at soup kitchens and Salvation Army shelters.

By 1932, twelve million people were jobless. Herbert Hoover had been the president for four years. In November, the scared and desperate American voters elected a new president, Franklin Delano Roosevelt, who promised a "new deal for the American people." Four days before his inauguration, Roosevelt announced his appointment of Frances Perkins as secretary of labor. The rest of his cabinet was made up of nine men, including Cordell Hull, secretary of state; Harold Ickes, secretary of the interior; and Henry Wallace, secretary of agriculture.

On March 4, 1933, Roosevelt was inaugurated. Because of the economic crisis, the Senate had quickly confirmed his cabinet appointments so that they could also be sworn in on the fourth. On Monday, March 6, Frances Perkins went to work.

"We were in a terrible situation," Perkins wrote years later. "Banks were closing. The economic life of the country was almost at a standstill." Since William Doak, the secretary of labor before Perkins, had not done very much to help jobless people in America, perhaps it was inevitable that cockroaches had moved into the secretary of labor's desk. But now Frances Perkins was taking over, and the cockroaches weren't welcome. Quickly she eliminated the roaches and got to work.

Frances Perkins, or Madam Secretary as she was called, knew that the American people were "gray and bleak and desperate." She was determined to find ways to end their suffering. And she did. Despite hate mail and harsh treatment by the press, her husband's chronic mental illness, and a resolution of impeachment against her, Frances Perkins successfully fought to make life better for working people by establishing unemployment insurance, minimum wages, maximum hours, safety regulations, and Social Security. A pioneer in labor reform, Frances Perkins served an extraordinary twelve years as secretary of labor, the second longest term of *any* cabinet member in history. Harold Ickes, Roosevelt's secretary of the interior, served only seven and a half months longer than Perkins.

During her lifetime, a time when women faced severe

restrictions and prejudices, Frances Perkins achieved many firsts—first woman head of an industrial commission, first woman in a governor's cabinet, first woman in a president's cabinet. But never without a public furor. "Fanny Perkins, Former Worcester Girl, Gets $8000 Job & Starts a Rumpus" read the newspaper headline in her hometown of Worcester, Massachusetts, when she was appointed the first woman member of the New York State Industrial Commission (a position that with its eight-thousand-dollar-a-year salary made her the highest-paid state official in the country). And when she was appointed secretary of labor, the editorial in the *Baltimore Sun* read, "A woman smarter than a man is something to get on guard about. But a woman smarter than a man and also not afraid of a man, well, good-night."

Fortunately, Frances Perkins wasn't raised by someone with the attitudes of the person who wrote the *Baltimore Sun* editorial. On the contrary, her parents encouraged her and her younger sister, Ethel, to be smart, to learn, to think, and to be unafraid. Her mother, Susie, a large woman, was artistic, energetic, and, according to a cousin, "not bashful about expressing her ideas." She was fun, and people liked being around her. Perkins always remembered how her mother could "sketch and draw anything" and how she would entertain the neighborhood children by modeling "horses, donkeys, cows" from clay.

Perkins's father, Fred, a slightly built man with bright blue eyes, was quiet and studious. He read poetry and plays written in Greek and discussed politics and law with his friends. Determined to share his knowledge, he began teaching Frances Greek grammar when she was about eight. According to Perkins, her father was the "sweetest looking person." When Perkins was about nine years old, her father went on a business trip and heard Dr. Anna Howard Shaw speak in favor of women's suffrage, or the right to vote. Perkins never forgot how her father raved about the speech. It was "the most wonderful speech I have ever heard," Fred Perkins told his wife and two daughters. "From that time on he was for woman's suffrage," Perkins remembered.

Perkins also never forgot her father teaching her about how to treat people: "How you must never overlook anyone . . . and how you must have a way, an approach to people with whom you talk, while not subservient, not arrogant," Perkins recalled.

Frances Perkins was born on April 10, 1880, in Boston, Massachusetts, almost fifteen years to the day after the Civil War ended. There were thirty-eight states in the United States, and Rutherford B. Hayes was the president. Cattle drives up the Chisholm Trail between Texas and Kansas were at a peak (by 1885, the cattle would travel by railroad). Elevated steam trains had started to run along Second, Third, Sixth, and Ninth avenues in New York City. Large numbers of immigrants continued to come to America and work in the growing number of low-paying factory jobs. According to the 1880 census, there were more than one hundred millionaires, a big jump up from the fewer than twenty reported in 1840. In November, James A. Garfield was elected president. And, on December 20, a mile of Broadway, the famous street in New York City, was lit up by a new type of electric light system instead of by gas lanterns.

Perkins was originally named Fannie Coralie Perkins—a name she changed to Fanny Perkins, then Frances C. Perkins, and finally, when she was twenty-five, to Frances Perkins, the name she used for the rest of her life, even after she married Paul Wilson. "My generation was perhaps the first that openly and actively asserted—at least some of us did—the separateness of women and their personal independence in the family relationship," Perkins once wrote.

Perkins came by her independence naturally. For as far

Frances Perkins, age four
(NATIONAL WOMEN'S HALL
OF FAME)

back as colonial times, her ancestors were hardworking farmers, merchants, and seafarers. Perkins was particularly proud of her relatives James Otis, the fiery revolutionary war patriot, and his sister, Mercy Otis Warren, the brilliant revolutionary war–era playwright. Then there was her great-aunt who ran off to marry the captain of a sailing vessel. Frances Perkins loved to hear the stories about how her aunt and the captain sailed far and wide together. Her favorite relative was her grandmother Cynthia Otis Perkins, "an extremely wise woman—worldly-wise as well as spiritually wise," Perkins said.

Frances Perkins spent her summers with her grandmother on the family farm in Newcastle, Maine. It was a wonderful place. There was a wooden carriage house, red barn, privy, icehouse, and farmhouse, called the Brick House, surrounded by maple trees and clumps of lilacs and barberries. A path led through a forest of oak and pine trees to a wide meadow along the banks of the Damariscotta River, where the Perkinses kept a canoe, rowboat, and sailboat. With blue eyes as bright as the brightest blue sky, snow white hair, and a wiry body, Cynthia Otis Perkins filled Frances Perkins's mind with pithy sayings and wise insights. "I am extraordinarily the product of my grandmother...," Perkins once wrote. "Scarcely a week goes by that I don't find myself saying, 'As my grandmother used to say,' and then repeating something that apparently has been a guiding principle all of my life."

During the rest of the year, Frances Perkins lived in Worcester, Massachusetts, where her family had moved when she was two. Originally inhabited by the Nipmuc Indians, Worcester was settled by white people in 1673 and named Quinsigamond. By the mid-1800s it was a thriving town with many factories and barges carrying goods along the Blackstone Canal which connected Worcester with Narragansett Bay and the Atlantic Ocean.

Perkins's father ran a profitable stationery store. Her mother managed a lively and friendly household. Periodically her sister, Ethel, broke the family peace with her temper tantrums. Kicking furniture, breaking dishes, slamming doors, Ethel erupted when she didn't get her way. Eventually Ethel learned to control herself. Watching Ethel figure out how to manage her emotions helped Frances Perkins years later when she dealt with politicians and business and labor leaders who thought they could get their way by ranting and raving. Frances Perkins just ignored them—if, as a youngster, her sister could learn to behave, so could grown-ups.

When Perkins was twelve years old, her mother bought

her a tricorn, or three-cornered hat. "My dear, that is your hat," Perkins recalled her mother saying. "You should always wear a hat something like it. You have a very broad face. Your head is actually narrower above the temples than it is at the cheekbones. Also, it slopes off very suddenly into your chin. . . . Never let yourself get a hat that is narrower than your cheekbones, because it makes you look ridiculous." As an adult, Perkins rarely appeared without a hat, and almost always it was a tricorn.

Although in some ways Perkins was shy (too shy to walk "into the public library to ask for a book or to go into a store to buy a spool of thread"), she loved to talk. Considering it unladylike for her to be a "talky child," her father set about to change her. "If you have anything to say, say it definitely, and stop," he would admonish her. Taking his lessons to heart, Perkins developed a crisp, direct way of speaking. Throughout her life, she would stop herself in midsentence if she thought she was "babbling" or interrupt when other people were talking on and on to ask, "Is that really important?"

Although Perkins lived a comfortable life, she was aware that other people didn't. "One of the girls who was among my best friends came from a poverty-stricken home. Her family was delightful and I used to wonder how such things could happen . . . ," Perkins recalled years later. When she asked her parents about poverty, they told her what most people of their time believed: that people were poor because they drank too much, because they were lazy, because they didn't save enough. . . . But those answers didn't make sense to Perkins. Her friends didn't drink, and they weren't lazy. And, so, she continued to wonder about why some people were poor and others weren't.

She also wondered about prejudice. As a young child she had seen a mob chasing a group of young Irish immigrants and screaming names at them. Perkins never forgot the terrified looks on the immigrants' faces or the vicious looks on the faces of the mob.

On June 20, 1898, Frances Perkins graduated from Worcester Classical High School, where she had been a star debater. It was the year in which America won the Spanish-American War and gained Puerto Rico, Guam, and the Philippines. It was a year in which new companies were formed—Goodyear Tire and Rubber, Union Carbide, Republic Steel, National Biscuit Co. Northeastern University was founded. Pepsi-Cola was introduced, as was a new cough medicine, which was named after its main ingredient—Heroin.

Perkins was almost five feet five inches tall. Her eyes were large and dark brown. She had an olive complexion, and wore

Worcester Classical High School, Worcester, Massachusetts. Perkins graduated in 1898. (PHOTOGRAPH FROM THE COLLECTIONS OF THE WORCESTER HISTORICAL MUSEUM, WORCESTER, MASSACHUSETTS)

her wavy brown hair in a single braid down her back. Although few girls went to college, Perkins's parents just assumed that she would go. So she enrolled in Mount Holyoke, a college for women in South Hadley, Massachusetts, not far from Worcester. Never a very serious student ("I could talk well and I successfully bluffed through," she once confessed), Perkins wasn't prepared to meet the demands of some of the professors she was about to encounter—Esther Van Dieman, Nellie Esther Goldthwaite, and Annah May Soule. But they were ready and waiting for her.

CHAPTER TWO

Perk

1898–1910

"I discovered for the first time ... that I had a mind."

$f$rances Perkins loved Mount Holyoke. The campus was beautiful—the stately, dark, redbrick buildings, majestic trees, two lakes, a stream with a pond, and an old stone mill. Although shy at first, Perkins was thoroughly involved before long. She cheered on the bloomer-clad members of the basketball team and participated in the literary club and in theatrical productions. By the time she was a senior, Perkins was elected the permanent class president and voted "the girl who has done the most for her class." Known as Perk, she was famous for her sense of humor, her pranks, and her ability to get things done.

Academically things weren't so easy for Perkins. Her first surprise was Professor Esther Van Dieman's first year Latin course. Determined to challenge Perkins, Dr. Van Dieman refused to let her slide by. She pushed Perkins to be absolutely accurate with her translations and to thoroughly understand the grammar. Almost correct wasn't good enough. Despite being pushed to tears, Perkins gradually realized that "for the first time I became conscious of character"—meaning her own character and how she handled difficult situations.

She continued to develop her character when she took a required chemistry course her second year. Finding herself in over her head, Perkins doubted that she could pass. But Professor Nellie Esther Goldthwaite "hounded" her until she mastered the material. Frances Perkins learned more than chemistry from Goldthwaite: "I discovered for the first time, under the stimulus of that course and of that teacher, that I had a mind," Perkins said. "My intellectual pride was aroused and the grim determination awakened in me to get the most I could out of college."

Perkins decided to major in chemistry with a minor in physics and biology. Although she never got high grades, she never regretted having to deal with "Dr. Goldthwaite's hounding personality, the pounding impact of her intelligence. . . ." In fact, when Perkins herself became a teacher, she advised students to "avoid snap courses; choose only the most strenuous, the most exacting; welcome mental discipline. . . ."

An American history course with Professor Annah May Soule taught Frances Perkins about another world—the world of factories and their workers.

Dr. Soule required that her students actually go to the factories in nearby Holyoke, Massachusetts, and conduct a survey of the working conditions. Although today, Dr. Soule's approach wouldn't be considered unusual, in her day, when historians focused on political and military events and not social, economic, or cultural ones, it was extraordinary. "We went to look at paper mills, textile mills . . . I was astonished and fascinated by what I saw," Perkins remembered.

In Holyoke, an industrial city built on the Connecticut River around a dam and canal system, Perkins discovered that men worked very long hours for very low wages. Women and children worked just as long, but for even lower wages. Some factories were dark and dank. Machines didn't have safety devices. Injuries were common, and, unlike today, there were no benefits or insurance for injured workers. There were no laws

A page from a test Perkins took in chemistry. At the bottom is a note from Dr. Nellie Esther Goldthwaite, the professor who "hounded" Perkins until she mastered the material. Goldthwaite wrote: "The average of your oral work falls much below your written work. N. E. G. [Nellie Esther Goldthwaite]" (MOUNT HOLYOKE COLLEGE ARCHIVES)

requiring employers to install safety devices or to maintain decent working conditions. Perkins took careful notes. She made a chart on which she recorded information including the nationalities of the workers, their hours and wages, and the company's earnings. She began to understand why factory workers were poor.

Perkins wasn't alone in her concern about factory conditions and working people. Throughout America people such as Ida Tarbell, Jane Addams, and Jacob Riis were speaking out for social, political, and economic reforms. They were pointing out with shocking statistics, vivid photographs, and strong words that although the astonishing growth of industry in America was amazing, it was also awful.

Amazing with such inventions as the telephone (1876, four years before Frances Perkins was born); the phonograph (1877, three years before her birth); the electric light (1879, one year before her birth); and the first airplane flight (1903, one year after Perkins graduated from college). But awful with rich business owners living in mansions on large estates and poor workers living in crowded tenements in city slums. Awful with big businesses taking over smaller businesses by illegal means. Awful with dishonest politicians and businessmen running city and state governments. Awful with children of all ages working long hours in factories. Awful with women working as hard as men but getting paid less. Awful with dangerous working conditions in most mines, factories, and sweatshops.

Perkins started her junior year at Mount Holyoke in 1900. Sugar cost four cents a pound, eggs fourteen cents a dozen, and a turkey dinner at a boarding house cost twenty cents. That same year, hamburgers were perfected at Louis Lunch in New Haven, Connecticut. The International Ladies Garment Workers Union was founded by women cloakmakers. There were 76 million Americans (in 1990 there were 248.7 million Americans). Trolley cars provided public transportation in cities. Bathtubs were found in one out of every seven American homes; showers were rare. A hurricane killed more than six thousand people in Galveston, Texas. William McKinley was the president. Big businesses were thriving, and businessmen had enormous financial and political power.

In the fall of Perkins's senior year, McKinley was assassinated and his vice president, Theodore Roosevelt, became president.

"Like many young people, I was an ardent admirer of Theodore Roosevelt," Perkins later remembered. What she liked about him were his "progressive ideas," or his ideas that everybody should get a "square deal" in America, not just big business owners. Like a growing number of Americans, Roosevelt thought it was time for reforms—time to put some limits on big business, to drive out corrupt politicians, to provide better opportunities for working people, and to improve conditions in the cities. "Out of the period that I was in school a whole generation, particularly women emerged, but men, too, who had a great passion for social justice," Perkins said years later.

During her senior year, Frances Perkins heard Florence Kelley speak. A dynamic, independent, passionate, and controversial social reformer known as a "raging furnace" about issues of social justice, Kelley had successfully fought to get laws passed in the state of Illinois to prohibit child labor and to limit the number of hours that women worked. According to Perkins, Kelley's speech, "first opened my mind to the necessity for and the possibility of the work which became my vocation."

In addition to Kelley's speech, Perkins was influenced by various books that exposed horrendous situations, including Jacob Riis's book *How the Other Half Lives,* an exposé of tenement life in New York City that "deeply moved" Perkins.

A strong religious faith undergirded Frances Perkins's concerns. "I was considerably religious minded," Perkins once said. She taught Sunday School and attended prayer meetings. For Perkins being religious meant that she had a "duty" to help people. She agreed with the words of Mary Lyon, the founder

On June 16, 1902, Perkins (left, front) *led the class of 1902 in the Ivy Exercise, a Mount Holyoke College tradition. Perkins carried a pot of ivy as she and her classmates marched to a spot on campus where they planted the ivy.* (MOUNT HOLYOKE COLLEGE ARCHIVES)

of Mount Holyoke, that people "should live for God and do something." For their class motto, Perkins and her classmates chose the passage from the Bible "be ye stedfast...." (I Corinthians 15:58)

Perkins was graduated in June 1902. It was the same year that Beatrix Potter published *The Tale of Peter Rabbit*. Crayola brand crayons were introduced, as were animal crackers and toy bears with moveable arms and legs (they were called Teddy, the nickname of President Roosevelt, who once refused to shoot

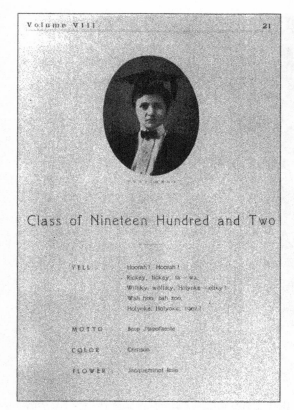

Volume VIII   21

Class of Nineteen Hundred and Two

YELL   Hoorah! Hoorah!
              Rickey, rickey, ta — wa,
              Williky, williky, Holyoke — oliky!
              Wah hoo, bah zoo,
              Holyoke, Holyoke, 1902!

MOTTO   Boop J'tapofacsle

COLOR   Crimson

FLOWER   Jacqueminot Rose

A page in The Llamar-
ada, *the Mount Holyoke
College yearbook, for the
class of 1902, with Per-
kins's picture as perma-
nent class president, and
the class yell, motto,
color, and flower* (MOUNT
HOLYOKE COLLEGE
ARCHIVES)

a mother bear during a hunting trip). It was also the year that a record number of immigrants came to America, mostly from Italy, Austria-Hungary, and Russia.

For two years, Perkins had various teaching jobs close to home. Then in 1904 she went to teach at Ferry Hall, a famous girls' school in Lake Forest, Illinois. Whenever she had free time, Perkins went into nearby Chicago to shop and go to the theater, art museum, and concerts. She also spent time at Hull House, founded by Jane Addams, and Chicago Commons, founded by Graham Taylor, two of America's most famous settlement houses, or houses in the slums where well-educated people like Perkins settled to share poor people's lives and help them improve their situation.

At Hull House and Chicago Commons, Perkins was immersed in the lives of people who wore ragged clothes, lived crowded together in rickety buildings, suffered from malnutrition and disease, and were paid what amounted to pennies for the hours they worked. It was an overwhelming experience. "What *is* the trouble? How *can* we cure this? . . . What *can* be done?" Frances Perkins wondered. Before long, Perkins decided to leave teaching: "I had to do something about unnecessary hazards to life, unnecessary poverty. It was sort of up to me. This feeling . . . sprang out of a period of great philosophical confusion which overtakes all young people," she wrote years later.

Determined to be a social worker, Perkins "wrote to anybody I knew who had any connection at all with charities to say I wanted a job, but had no experience." Her friend Rachel Reilly in Boston wrote to her about a job in Philadelphia with the Philadelphia Research and Protective Association, a new organization that had been formed by concerned citizens to investigate rumors that pimps, thieves, and unscrupulous employers were preying on newly arrived immigrant girls and young black women from the South. Perkins applied, was hired, and moved to Philadelphia in the fall of 1907 (after she spent a "lazy summer" in Italy where she filled a sketch pad with pencil drawings).

Her job was to check out the rumors and "find the facts," she later explained. "If the facts were found, I was to devise ways to prevent it or overcome it either by social representation or by legislation at the municipal or state level."

Armed with her notebook and pencil, Perkins investigated all aspects of the situation—lodging houses, transportation facilities, wages, employment offices, types of jobs, social connections, and the legal system. "Ten cent lodging houses, employment agencies, the offices of the Philadelphia political 'gangs,' and the two police courts all became my haunts," Perkins wrote to her classmates in a class letter that was published in the *Mount Holyoke Alumnae Quarterly.*

Perkins worked hard. She uncovered a variety of abuses and devised programs to help the young women. She lobbied officials to get regulations and legislation passed. In addition, she gave speeches to inform people and raise money, discovering that she had a "talent" for making speeches. "I had a good voice and a strong one," she later noted.

She also discovered that she "knew so little about the whole field of social work." Of course, not many people knew much because the idea of social work and social workers was very new. As Perkins once said, "Social work was an infant then." Determined to learn what was known, Perkins took night courses at the University of Pennsylvania from Professor Simon Patten. A leading economist, Patten was famous for his idea of "surplus civilization," or the belief that with industrialization there would be enough money for every person to have a decent life.

"I just lapped it up there," Perkins said later about her studies. "I discovered . . . that I had a mind that starts, operates on its own scheme, inquires, penetrates, goes to the bottom of things, puts two and two together and comes to some logical conclusions that have authority."

Life in Philadelphia was stimulating and challenging for Perkins. It was also difficult. Earning a meager salary, she periodically had to pawn her watch. She also endured periods of intense introspection: "And best (or worst) of all, I grew old during that time, so that now I am a settled and mature old spinster with an opinion on every topic under heaven. . . . I've also acquired . . . a sense of humor—so that I no longer take myself and my doings seriously," Perkins wrote to her classmates.

After two years in Philadelphia, Perkins had gained a good

Perkins as a young woman (MOUNT HOLYOKE COLLEGE ARCHIVES)

reputation for her work and was offered a scholarship to study at the New York School of Philanthropy in New York City. At the same time, she planned to get a master's degree in political science at Columbia University.

Perkins had been in New York City before. "I was badly bitten by the idea that I could have a place in the theatre," Perkins said. She had had a lot of theater experience at Mount Holyoke and she "had been good at it." She spent a summer in New York trying to get a job. However, no one would even talk to her. There were very few theater jobs open to women.

"I harbored that idea for a little while. It would have been a great pleasure, but I soon dropped it because I got a princi-ple . . . ," Perkins later explained. There was no doubt in Per-kins's mind—she had to devote herself to improving life for workers and poor people.

New York City was a thrilling place to be for a budding

social worker. "I am in the very heart of both the theoretical and practical efforts to socialize the life of the modern city," Perkins wrote to a friend. "Good people were rising out of the population then.... The movement was humane and religious and the beginning of the appreciation that we were a very rich country and that we didn't have to take these chances," she later recalled.

As part of her studies, Perkins conducted a survey of undernourished children in Hell's Kitchen, a district as tough as its name in New York City. Unafraid, Perkins took her notebook and pencil and conducted her investigation. Along the way, she met Thomas MacManus, known as The MacManus. A state senator and political boss of Hell's Kitchen, MacManus was part of Tammany Hall, a group of powerful and corrupt political leaders in New York City.

Perkins had been warned about MacManus and his power, which is why she marched into his office one day seeking help for a young boy. The sole supporter of his mother and sisters, the boy was in police custody. His mother had tried to get help from a charity organization but was turned away. When Perkins heard about the situation, she boldly and bravely went to see MacManus.

"It was one of these typical, very roughneck, Tammany headquarters with a lot of people milling around, a lot of big talk, smoke, spitting.... I asked to see Mr. MacManus and was told, 'Sure, lady, he'll be glad to see you,'" Perkins later recalled.

MacManus listened to Perkins and told her to return the next day. She did and MacManus told her the boy had been released. "I don't know what he did or how he did it. I was too innocent to know," Perkins remembered.

As Perkins always did, she thought about what had happened. Clearly MacManus wasn't all bad. Clearly he could get things done that Perkins cared about. Clearly the charitable organization had refused to help the boy. Perhaps people and organizations weren't all good or all bad, all right or all wrong. While Perkins never forgot the corrupt part of MacManus, she also did not hesitate to seek his help when she needed it.

In 1910, Perkins received her master's degree and published her first article, "Some Facts Concerning Certain Undernourished Children." She also was hired as the executive secretary of the New York City Consumers' League, a chapter of the National Consumers' League.

The National Consumers' League, founded in 1899 by Florence Kelley, Josephine Shaw Lowell and John Graham Brooks, was organized to "awaken consumers to their responsibility for the conditions under which the goods they buy are made and sold." By conducting inspections and investigations, collecting statistics, and taking photographs, the Consumers' League gathered information about sanitary conditions, safety, wages, and hours. Then it published detailed reports with such titles as *Behind the Scenes in a Restaurant* and *Less Than a Living Wage,* and a White List with the names of shops, stores, and factories that met the League's standards. League members gave speeches, wrote articles, testified before various committees and legislatures, and lobbied for improved working conditions and the end of child labor. The League's slogan was "investigate, agitate, legislate."

Florence Kelley, the woman whose speech eight years earlier had inspired Perkins, was executive secretary, or head, of the National Consumers' League when Perkins was hired as executive secretary of the New York City branch. Both women lived in New York—Kelley at the Henry Street Settlement House and Perkins at the Greenwich House, another settlement house—and were closely involved with other passionate reformers—Lillian Wald, Mary Dreier, and Rose Schneiderman.

Although she knew Kelley "was no gentle saint" to work

with, Perkins was eager to join forces with her. With her tricorn hat centered in the middle of her broad forehead above her expressive brown eyes, Frances Perkins plunged into her work. Finally, at the age of thirty, she was a trained and experienced social worker. She was determined to do her duty, no matter how difficult it was. Little did she know how hard things could get.

CHAPTER THREE

Something Had to Be Done

1910–1918

*"I felt I must sear it not only on my mind but
on my heart. . . ."*

*I*n October 1910, Frances Perkins set out to survey the bakery
business in New York City. Were bread, rolls, donuts rolled
on clean breadboards? Were there proper ventilation and light
for the workers? Did the workers have decent hours and wages?
Were there insects and rodents in the bakeries?

Armed with her notebook and pencil, Perkins personally
visited a hundred bakeries. She enlisted a group of volunteers
who visited hundreds more. Their discoveries made consumers
think twice about the bread they were eating. For, according to
Perkins's detailed report, most of the bakeries were in cellars
where rats frolicked around bags of flour, cats had kittens on
the breadboards, and there was filth everywhere. The New York
Consumers' League presented the bakery report with recommendations to the Board of Health, and urged consumers to
push for regulations. As a result, conditions improved.

Next, Perkins turned her attention to fire safety. Determined to learn everything she could about fire prevention, Perkins talked to engineers, fire fighters, architects, and anyone else

she could find who knew about sprinkler systems, fire escapes, exits, and fire hazards. And she investigated factories and climbed rickety fire escapes, crawled into narrow passages, measured the width of corridors, and thoroughly checked out every place she visited. All too often she discovered that fire escapes were unsafe, sprinkler systems rarely installed, fire exits frequently inaccessible, and that most of the factories in New York City were located in lofts above the seventh floor, far beyond the reach of fire truck ladders.

Frances Perkins knew that it was just a matter of time before a disaster burst into flames.

And it did, on March 25, 1911, not far from where Perkins was having tea with some friends. Hearing clanging fire bells and the clattering of hooves as horses pulled the fire engines through the street, Perkins and her friends rushed to the door. In horror they saw flames and smoke raging through the top floors of the Asch Building, at the corner of Washington Place and Greene Street, where the Triangle Shirtwaist Company was located.

A year before Triangle workers had gone on strike. Two of their key demands were fire escapes that worked and unlocked doors. Instead of talking to the strikers, the owners hired scabs, or new workers who agreed not to strike. Without any way to earn a living, the strikers finally gave up and returned to work. Now they were trapped behind doors that were locked to keep the union organizers out and the workers in.

"Without saying much of anything, we all went down the steps and just went toward the fire. . . . It was the most horrible sight. . . . People were hanging out of the windows by their hands. . . . One by one, the people would fall off. . . . People who had their clothes afire would jump," Perkins recalled.

No one survived the fall. Fire horses whinnied in terror and strained at their harnesses to escape the screams and sounds of bodies hitting the pavement. Some bodies hit with such a force that they cracked through the sidewalk. A newspaper reporter at the scene wrote, "The floods of water from the firemen's hoses that ran into the gutter were actually red with blood." The final death toll was 146 workers, all but fifteen of them girls and young women.

The scene "struck at the pit of my stomach," Perkins wrote years later. "I felt I must sear it not only on my mind but on my heart as a never-to-be-forgotten reminder of why I had to spend my life fighting conditions that could permit such a tragedy."

More than 3,500 people attended a mass meeting after the fire. Frances Perkins was there. So was Rose Schneiderman, a garment worker and leader of the Women's Trade Union League. A tiny woman with fiery red hair, Schneiderman ad-

Victims of the Triangle Shirtwaist Company fire of 1911, who fell to their deaths. Perkins was at the scene of the fire and vowed to fight for safer working conditions. (TAMIMENT INSTITUTE LIBRARY, NEW YORK UNIVERSITY)

dressed the crowd, "I would be a traitor to those poor burned bodies, if I were to come here to talk good fellowship. . . . This is not the first time girls have been burned alive in this city. Every week I must learn of the untimely death of one of my sister workers.

"Every year thousands of us are maimed. The life of men and women is so cheap and property is so sacred! There are so many of us for one job, it matters little if 140-odd are burned to death. . . ."

The public outcry was tremendous—an estimated 120,000 women, children, and men marched up Fifth Avenue in a funeral procession for seven unidentified victims. Ignoring the cold rain that fell all day, another four hundred thousand people lined the streets. There was no music. No noise. Just silence. And the sound of footsteps on the wet pavement.

In response to the fire, two major committees were formed. The first one, the Committee on Safety of the City of New York, was formed by New York City citizens shortly after the fire. The second one, the New York State Factory Investigating Commission, was formed by the state legislature on June 30, 1911. Two men who were to be an important part of Perkins's life, state senators Robert F. Wagner and Al Smith, were appointed the chair and vice chair of the commission. There were also four members from the legislature and four private citizens including Simon Brentano, a publisher and bookseller, and Mary Dreier, the president of the Women's Trade Union League who had been arrested in 1909 for participating in a strike of shirtwaist makers. During the summer and fall of 1911, Perkins advised both groups and served as an expert witness.

She also continued her work with the New York Consumers' League. Part of her job involved speaking to various organizations. On one occasion she traveled across the Hudson River to Englewood, New Jersey, where she spoke to a civic

Perkins about 1911, as an investigator of factories for the New York State Factory Investigating Commission. She is standing beside a fire escape ladder. (NATIONAL WOMEN'S HALL OF FAME)

group. As usual, she had a typed outline of her speech, which included: A. Women and the School, B. Women and Municipal Housekeeping, C. Women and Public Protection of Children. In the margin of her outline, Perkins scrawled additional comments in pencil, "We must have the *courage* to meddle. It is our business. It is not enough to manage your own household well. Your household is in danger so long as illness and hunger and poverty and crime endure in the community."

The need for child labor laws to prohibit employers from hiring young children was a subject Perkins spoke about frequently. "These children were working sixty to seventy-two hours a week in rush season in industries full of dust and fumes. The death rate was very high," Perkins told her audiences. And she ended her speeches by reciting "Little Toilers," a poem by Sara N. Claghorn, which ended with the verse:

27

The golf links lie so near the mills,
That nearly every day,
The laboring children can look out
And see the men at play.

Perkins did a lot of lobbying, in particular, on behalf of the fifty-four-hour bill (today the standard work week is forty hours), which would limit the number of hours women of all ages and boys under eighteen years old could work. Since January 1911, Perkins had been traveling to the state capitol in Albany to lobby legislators. Finally in March 1912, the vote on the bill was scheduled just before the legislature was due to adjourn. The vote was going to be close. Too close. Trying everything she could think of, Perkins asked for help from Senator Tim Sullivan, an intimidating and powerful politician known as Big Tim. Listening to her arguments, Big Tim said, "Me sister was a poor girl, and she went out to work when she was young. I feel kinda sorry for them poor girls that work the way you say they work. I'd like to do them a good turn. I'd like to do you a good turn." After casting his vote for the bill, Big Tim left to catch a boat for a trip down the Hudson River to his home in New York City. However, taking advantage of his absence, opponents to the bill managed to defeat it.

But Frances Perkins refused to quit. Urging a supporter to get the bill reconsidered, she raced to a phone, hoping to catch Big Tim before the boat left. She did, and before long Big Tim returned. "It's all right, me girl," he gasped to Perkins as he struggled to catch his breath. "We is with you." Using his influence, Big Tim persuaded enough senators to change their vote and the bill passed. "You pulled a smart one," Senator Al Smith told Perkins later. "That was very smart. I didn't think you had the courage to do it."

In getting the fifty-four-hour bill passed, Perkins was disappointed in the actions of young politician Franklin Roosevelt.

Although Roosevelt later claimed that he helped get the fifty-four-hour bill passed, Perkins knew that he hadn't. In fact, he had brushed her off when she had asked him to support the bill. At the time Perkins had no idea how Roosevelt would eventually affect her life.

In May 1912, Perkins resigned from the New York Consumers' League (although she stayed involved and she was elected to its board of directors) and went to work full time for the Committee on Safety, which was working closely with the Factory Investigating Commission. Now that the fifty-four-hour bill had passed, she wanted to concentrate on making factories safer.

"I was much younger than anybody on the commission and not a personage in New York at all, but I did know a great deal about the subject.... I was constantly being called as a witness about fire, about accidents, about sanitation," Perkins remembered.

Perkins took commission members on factory tours throughout New York. She took Al Smith, who later became governor of New York,

> to see the women, thousands of them, coming off the ten-hour night shift on the rope walks in Auburn. We made sure that Robert Wagner personally crawled through the tiny hole in the wall that gave egress to a steep iron ladder covered with ice and ending twelve feet from the ground, which was euphemistically labeled "Fire Escape" in many factories. We saw to it that the austere legislative members of the Commission got up at dawn and drove with us for an unannounced visit to a Cattaraugus County cannery and that they saw with their own eyes the little children, not adolescents, but five-, six-, and seven-year-olds, snipping beans and shelling peas. We made sure that they saw the machinery that would scalp a girl or cut off a man's arm. Hours so long that both men and women were de-

pleted and exhausted became realities to them through seeing for themselves the dirty little factories.

Seeing for themselves had a powerful effect on the members of the Factory Investigating Commission. Perkins helped write the commission's final report and recommendations. As a result of the commission's work, New York State became a leader in improving sanitation, safety, and working conditions. Thirty-three laws were passed, including ones that limited the age of children at work and provided workmen's compensation, or money for workers who were injured at work.

"The extent to which this legislation in New York marked a change in American political attitudes and policies toward social responsibility can scarcely be overrated. It was, I am convinced, a turning point . . . ," Perkins later said.

Ironically, although Frances Perkins was immersed in politics and legislation, as a woman she couldn't vote. Perkins worked with other suffragists to change this absurd state of affairs. In the process, she became a skilled street-corner speaker. Standing on a wooden grocery box beside a banner proclaiming "Women's Suffrage," Perkins learned to speak in spite of hecklers, horn honkers, and traffic noises. The experience "did more to make me truly at ease with everybody . . . ," Perkins once noted. "I learned the advantage of a little funny story—very short, very pointed, very harmless, not derogatory to anybody. . . . It's a trick that's stood by me many times. If the crowd laughs with you once, they're for you and not for the fellow who's bothering you."

Perkins also marched in women's suffrage parades, including the Great Suffrage Parade in New York City on October 23, 1915. Wearing suffrage colors of gold, purple, and white, twenty-four thousand women and about two thousand men paraded up Fifth Avenue from where it begins in Greenwich Village at Washington Square to Fifty-Ninth Street, where Central Park begins. A quarter of a million spectators watched and cheered as marching bands, women on horseback, and automobiles passed by. As incredible as it may seem to modern readers, Frances Perkins wasn't able to vote until 1917 (by then she was thirty-seven years old!), when women finally won the right to vote in New York State. Three years later, women won the right to vote in national elections when the Nineteenth Amendment was ratified, or approved, by enough states to make it part of the U.S. Constitution.

While she was fighting for the vote, Perkins made wonderful friendships. "The women learned to like each other in that suffrage movement.... They played fair with each other, supported each other...," Perkins remembered. "These people were the people who would stand by me when I was in trouble after I got to be a public officer many years later."

Meanwhile, on September 26, 1913, Frances Perkins married Paul Wilson. "I wasn't very anxious to get married," Perkins explained years later. "To tell the truth, I was reluctant." But, as she continued to explain, "I thought I better marry and get it off my mind, because I was always being challenged by somebody who thought he should marry me or wanted to recommend the institution.... I finally thought, 'I better marry. I know Paul Wilson well. I like him....'"

An intelligent, handsome man, Wilson was an economist and an expert on the financial situation of New York City. Like Perkins, he was committed to social reforms. Their two-floor house at 121 Washington Place West in New York City was a swirl of activity. Friends stayed for various periods of time. Colleagues dropped by for discussions that sometimes lasted all night.

Shortly after their marriage, Wilson was hired by the newly elected mayor of New York, John Purroy Mitchel. "My husband has a stake in the present New York City administration," Perkins wrote in a class letter, "... a number of other personal friends are also involved in it.... Lots of fun! and sometimes gives one quite a sense of being on the switchboard of contemporary history."

Perkins hired a German couple as live-in help. In her usual organized fashion, she typed up a "Daily Program" of duties that included:

1. Brush front door and pillars
2. Rub up brass very quickly
3. Brush off iron window-rails
4. Water the trees
5. 7:45 o'clock, knock on door of our room—papers, letters etc.

. . .

7. Set breakfast table. Have coffee service ready and fruit on table before we come down. Have trays ready. Clean apron, cap and collar.

Going completely against tradition, Perkins did not change her name to Wilson. It was a decision that she had to defend time and time again. And she did so in no uncertain terms. On one occasion she wrote to the Mount Holyoke Alumnae Association, "Letters from women who do not know me by sight and who cannot possibly know of or care about my marriage come addressed to me under my husband's name. I, therefore, think that some meddlesome person has told you to change my name on your records. I do not use my husband's name either socially or professionally and it makes a great deal of trouble and annoyance to have my mail so addressed. Please change your records...."

The year Perkins got married was also the year Woodrow Wilson was inaugurated president. In his inaugural speech, Wilson spoke words that Perkins surely agreed with:

We have been proud of our industrial achievements, but we have not hitherto stopped thoughtfully enough to count the human cost, the cost of lives snuffed out, of energies overtaxed and broken, the fearful physical and spiritual cost to the men and women and children upon whom the dead weight and burden of it all has fallen pitilessly the years through.... The great government we loved has too often been made use of for private and selfish purposes.... Our cry has been "Let every man look out for himself, let every generation look out for itself," while we reared giant machinery which made it impossible that any but those who stood at the levers of control should have a chance to look out for themselves.

In order to help workers, Wilson proposed a new cabinet office, the United States Department of Labor, which Congress created in 1913.

Perkins continued to work long hours with the Committee on Safety and the Factory Investigating Commission. But she also found "lots of odd moments for personal interests and artistic pursuits," she wrote in her class letter. "The Woman's Peace Movement, the promotion of Isadora Duncan's School of Dancing, the propaganda for limitation of families, wrestling with some of the more disagreeable phases of the problem of unemployment in New York City, keeping up with the post-impressionist school of painting and trying to raise bulbs in a New York back yard..."

She and Paul also had a "shack" on Long Island Sound. "I beat it to the country religiously every Saturday afternoon.... A weekly swim in the summer and a walk in the woods in the winter keeps me straight," Perkins wrote.

On December 30, 1916, Frances Perkins gave birth to a daughter, Susanna. She settled into raising Susanna. She also did volunteer work. In particular, she organized and ran the Maternity Center Association, an organization that provided care for pregnant women and infants. She also paid close attention to news about the war that had been raging in Europe since 1914.

So far, America had stayed out of the war. But now it seemed likely that America would join the fight. And it did, on April 19, 1917, when President Wilson asked Congress to declare war against Germany. All over America, people scrambled to get ready to fight World War I. Soldiers were recruited and trained. Equipment was manufactured. Supplies were assembled. Once war was declared, Perkins, who had worked hard for peace, volunteered to coordinate relief efforts in New York City.

That same year Al Smith, the former vice chair of the Factory Investigating Commission, ran for governor. It was the first New York State election in which women could vote. Knowing that Smith was a committed reformer, Perkins campaigned hard for him. In particular she focused on women voters. Treat women as serious, intelligent, concerned voters, Perkins advised Smith. And he did.

In November 1918, Smith won the election. About that same time, Paul Wilson developed what Perkins once described as "an up and down illness. He was sometimes depressed, sometimes excited. . . . Sometimes he was hospitalized, sometimes not." Wilson never fully recovered or worked regularly again.

Frances Perkins never talked about Wilson's illness. Nor did she bother with self-pity or despair. Instead she set about "to hustle to find things to do that would see us through. . . ." Then, suddenly, a few weeks after he was inaugurated in January 1919, Smith summoned Perkins to Albany, the state capital. Perkins thought he wanted to discuss a child labor law. Smith, however, had something else in mind.

CHAPTER FOUR

Extraordinary Energy

1919–1928

"Doing means digging your nails in and working like a truck horse."

*F*rances Perkins took the early morning train, the Empire State Express, from New York City to Albany to meet with Governor Al Smith.

When she arrived in his office, Smith said, "I was thinking. How would you like to be a member of the Industrial Commission of the State of New York?"

"Just like that with no preliminaries, no dancing up to it, no ifs, ands or buts," Perkins recalled.

The commission was responsible for supervising factory inspectors, setting health and safety standards, mediating disputes, and for making final decisions about awarding workmen's compensation to injured workers. No woman had served on the Industrial Commission, and Perkins was "tongue-tied for a moment."

Smith explained his reasons for appointing Perkins. First, the Industrial Commission was in terrible shape and needed a strong member to shake it up. Second, he knew that he could trust Perkins to do the right thing. Finally, Smith explained, it was time to appoint a woman because, "Women are going to vote from now on."

Before she agreed to serve, Perkins wanted to check with her mentor, Florence Kelley. She was worried that Kelley might not approve of her going to work for the government. By working outside of government, Perkins said, "I could be brave. . . . I have no political commitments. I didn't have to protect anybody. I could speak out openly. . . . I was serving the law and my God."

Perkins met Kelley the next day and asked for her opinion. To Perkins's surprise, Kelley's "eyes opened wide, her mouth opened, tears ran down her cheeks, as she said in a shaky voice 'Glory be to God! I never thought I would live to see the day when someone that we had trained, who knew about industrial conditions, cared about women, cared to have things right, would have the chance to be an administrative officer.' "

"Well, you know, Mrs. Kelley, there are going to be an awful lot of mistakes made. I'm going to make some of them. . . . Will I get hit over the head by the reformers for that?" Perkins asked.

"Not if you make an honest try," Kelley replied.

When Smith announced his appointment of Perkins, the reaction was fierce. Manufacturers wanted a businessperson appointed. Organized labor, or labor unions, wanted a union person appointed. One senator said that Perkins was nothing but an agitator.

Smith refused to back down. "The appointment of Miss Perkins will be confirmed [by the New York State Senate] all right, make no mistake about that. I appointed Miss Perkins because of her known ability and her knowledge of labor conditions. I also think that the millions of working girls in the State should be represented by at least one woman on the commission," Smith announced.

Despite the furor, Perkins was confirmed on February 18,

1919, by a vote of thirty-four to sixteen. That same year Germany signed the Treaty of Versailles, officially ending World War I. The Nineteenth Amendment granting women suffrage was adopted by Congress and sent to the states for ratification. Congress also established Grand Canyon National Park. Labor strikes and race riots erupted across America. The U.S. Attorney General A. Mitchell Palmer instigated a "Red Scare" and approved of mass arrests and deportations of people who were accused of being under "foreign influences." The Eighteenth Amendment to the Constitution prohibiting the sale of alcoholic beverages anywhere in the United States was ratified.

Perkins was concerned about how to approach her fellow commission members. After all, she later explained, "I had been the witness who stood on the stand before the Factory Investigating Commission and criticized in great detail the whole workings of the Industrial Commission." She confessed her concern to Abram Elkus, who had been the lawyer for the Factory Commission. "Just go in boldly," Elkus advised her. "Smile as though nothing had happened. . . . After all, they're all politicians."

Perkins had already learned a lot about dealing with politicians. Several years earlier, she had gained an invaluable insight from an encounter with Hugh Frawley, a state senator in Albany. Perkins described Frawley as "one of the most picturesque people that I ever saw in politics." A huge man with a big head of hair, Frawley always wore a bright pink shirt, oversized navy blue bow tie with large white polka dots, and a plaid waistcoat with a gold watch in the pocket that was attached to three yards of gold chain that had charms hanging from it. To complete his attire, he wore lots of jewelry and rings.

One day, while Perkins was lobbying legislators in Albany, she had bumped into Frawley. At the time, he was head of a committee that was investigating the governor.

"He grabbed me by the hand, he wrung it, and he began

to sort of gasp and said, 'Oh, Miss Perkins. We've done a terrible thing!' " Perkins later recalled. Sobbing and carrying on, Frawley told Perkins that his committee had just voted to impeach the governor. "I tried to save him myself. . . . It's so dreadful!" Frawley wailed and wiped his face with his handkerchief. "Every man's got a mother, you know."

"At first I thought it was funny," Perkins said later. "I told it to one or two intimates as funny and they thought it was funny, too." Then, as Perkins always did, she reflected about the experience. Since she and Frawley weren't friends, she wondered, why did he confide in her?

Finally, Perkins concluded it was because Frawley "thought of me as a good woman and that I wouldn't go around making sport of him. . . . I learned from this that the way men take women in political life is to associate them with motherhood. They know and respect their mothers—ninety-nine percent of them do. It's a primitive and primary attitude. I said to myself, 'That's the way to get things done. So behave, so dress, and so comport yourself that you remind them subconsciously of their mothers.' It was not long afterwards that I adopted the black dress with the bow of white at the throat as kind of an official uniform. It has always worked," Perkins later explained.

Governor Smith had said that Perkins would earn her high salary. And she did. When she started, the commission "hardly functioned." So Perkins met with the staff, including the factory inspectors, and reviewed their work. She got her fellow commissioners to hold regular meetings, and she pushed them to be responsible.

It was not easy. In one situation, she and her fellow commissioners discovered that a doctor was taking kickbacks from insurance companies to deny or limit claims from injured workers. So they met to decide what to do about the doctor who had been cheating workers. "I've never forgotten it because the pat-

Frances Perkins (MOUNT HOLYOKE COLLEGE ARCHIVES)

tern has been repeated over and over again in public life. Here were four grown men and me sitting at this table unable to make any progress at all and for the most part saying nothing. . . . One person would make a little statement about what a good man Dr. Blank had been . . . a man of estimable character, with highest morals. . . . Then they would all say yes. . . . Then we would begin all over. . . . This went on, and on, and on, until eleven o'clock. . . ."

Finally, Perkins nudged the commissioner sitting next to her. He was close to her age, and she thought he might help her get things moving. But, no, he wasn't bothered by the process.

"I remember thinking to myself, 'Do men really behave like this?' Women don't behave like this . . . women always have something else to do besides the business that is before the committee. . . . They've got to get home and wash the baby's shirt, if nothing else. . . . The habit of prolonged deliberation for no reason at all except that they haven't got the nerve to take action is more on the male side than it is on the female side in my observation. That was the first time I noted it," Perkins reflected years later.

Soon after her appointment, Perkins got a telephone call from John Flynn, a labor organizer. Flynn told her about a strike of copper workers in Rome, New York, that had been going on for months. The workers were striking against all five of the copper factories in Rome. They wanted an eight-hour day and the same wages that were being paid to copper workers in other states. But factory owners were refusing to talk to them.

The men were having a rough time, nobody was doing anything for them, Flynn told her. Perkins checked with Packy Downey, a labor mediator who worked for the Bureau of Mediation and Arbitration, part of the Industrial Commission. Downey agreed that the situation was serious. There could be violence.

"As a result of my talk with Flynn and Downey, I went out to spy out the land. The other members of the commission didn't think it was necessary, but I felt I had to go," Perkins said. Governor Smith agreed with her decision.

On July 15, 1919, Perkins took the night train to Rome. Before she boarded, she bought the late evening newspaper and read that there had been violence in Rome. John Spargo, one of the owners, drove his car through a group of strikers. When they tried to stop him, Spargo fired a gun into the crowd. "I read that before I went to bed. That was a pretty piece of news," Perkins recalled.

The next morning she discovered that Packy Downey was on the same train. The porter and conductor told them it was too dangerous to get off at Rome, but Perkins and Downey went anyhow. To get into town, they had to drive across a bridge that was blocked by angry strikers.

"It was the time when they still had these automobiles that you could push back the tops," Perkins later recalled. "Packy said [to the driver], 'You better put the top back so that we can stand up and they can see who we are.'"

The driver drove to the middle of the bridge and stopped before a human blockade of strikers. The leader of the men, who had rocks in their hands, moved toward the car.

"You all know me. I'm the mediator from Albany. This is the industrial commissioner," Downey said.

Perkins made a short speech and reassured the strikers that she was there to look into their problems. Then the strikers moved aside to let their car go across the bridge.

The most immediate problem was that the employers and their lawyer had convinced Governor Smith to call out the state police. By the time Perkins arrived, the police were already on the outskirts of Rome. "State police were in formation on their horses, on foot, in the kind of vans they moved in," Perkins remembered. The strikers were determined to fight back. And, Flynn nervously confided to Perkins, they had dynamite.

Knowing that she was taking a "terrible responsibility" on herself, Perkins decided not to tell Smith about the dynamite for fear that he might send in the state police to try to find the dynamite. She also decided to try to convince him to remove the state police all together. After several phone calls, Perkins succeeded. Then she went into the town square. People, most of whom were Italian immigrants, were sitting everywhere. They listened to the sounds of the state police leaving.

"They heard the horses clap, clap, clap out of town. They knew they were going," Perkins said later. As Perkins walked through the square many people called out, "Oh, la signora!" So, she stood on a bench and made a speech using the few Italian words she knew. "We are going to try to have law and order. I want everybody to cooperate," Perkins said.

That night Perkins and Flynn went with a striker named

Ludovicci to two houses. Ludovicci did most of the talking in Italian. He told the people gathered there that Perkins knew they had dynamite and that she had promised the governor that they would get rid of it if the state police left.

Perkins watched as the men disappeared into the basement. "They came up with their loads in suitcases, bags, and various other things—I remember one man put it on a baby carriage— one by one, two by two, they went over toward the canal and dumped it in. It was extraordinary," Perkins recalled.

Finally Perkins got three other commission members to agree to hold an official hearing in Rome on August 4. They met in the courthouse. Every seat was taken. The balcony was packed. There were people on the steps, standing on the big windowsills, in the park across the street. First the workers testified. Then the employers spoke through their lawyers.

"This, of course, is another thing that annoys the working people beyond words," Perkins later observed. "Grown men who own the factories won't say for themselves what they think, and what they will do, but shut their mouths tight, look at the floor and get a lawyer to do their talking for them."

Unable to get the owners to talk with the workers, Perkins met privately with the other commissioners. She showed them a letter that Flynn had given to her. It was a nasty letter full of foul language that John Spargo, the owner who had fired his gun at the crowd of strikers, had sent to the strikers. The letter had greatly offended the strikers. Although the other owners had not read Spargo's letter, they had heard about it and were greatly embarrassed. They were glad when the letter seemed to disappear.

Unfortunately for the owners, the letter had disappeared into the bottom of Perkins's purse. And, now, she convinced her fellow commissioners that it was time to read the letter in public. In a day when people were offended by foul language, especially when women were present, that was too much for the owners. In exchange for not having the letter read in public, the owners agreed to negotiate with the workers. The strike was over. Celebrated as heros by the strikers and the owners, Perkins and her colleagues left town "in a blaze of glory."

Perkins gave Smith a full report, including the incident with the dynamite. "You sure had your nerve. It was risky business," Smith told her. Then he congratulated her.

In 1920, Smith ran for reelection and was defeated. When Perkins's term expired in April 1921, the new governor appointed another commissioner to replace her. Perkins got a job as executive director of the Council on Immigrant Education, where she organized programs to help newly arrived immigrants adjust to life in America. She missed being a commissioner and later described this time in her life as "a drudgery and keep-your-nose-to-the-grindstone period."

Smith ran for governor again in 1922. Perkins prepared position papers for him on labor issues, gave speeches, and organized women voters. Smith won in a landslide. Since Smith's previous term in office, the Industrial Commission had been reorganized. Now there was an industrial commissioner, or head executive officer, who administered the New York State Department of Labor and an Industrial Board with three commissioners. The Industrial Board had basically the same range of duties as the former Industrial Commission, including administrating labor law, formulating health and safety codes, and deciding workmen's compensation cases.

"I am, as some of you know, reappointed by Gov. Smith to my old post as Commissioner of the State Industrial Board, and am happy and interested with hard and important work to do," Perkins wrote that year in her class letter. She also wrote, "My little girl grows tall and strong and nice."

It was rare for Perkins to comment about her family. She

was a private person and had little use for questions about her personal life. When the editor of the *Mount Holyoke Alumnae Quarterly* wrote to her asking for her opinion about "the subject of marriage with or without a career for the college woman," Perkins returned the letter with her response scrawled in black ink on the back:

> I haven't responded because the subject seemed rather silly and obvious. The kind of thing the "woman's pages" of a newspaper discusses.
>
> I really have no "views" on the subject. A woman *can* marry & work if she has to or *really wants* to. She can't if talking about it is the principle emotional or intellectual factor in the situation. Otherwise the variations are as infinite as the variations of personality.

In 1926, Smith appointed Perkins chairperson of the Industrial Board. "Miss Frances Perkins Is First of Her Sex for Office in Empire State" read the headline for a newspaper article. The article went on to state that "Miss Perkins, more than any individual in our State, knows the conditions under which labor may function to the best advantage of employer and employee." In response to the reporter's question about people who say they want to improve conditions but just can't find anything to do, Perkins responded, "Doing means digging your nails in and working like a truck horse. We make most of our own opportunities. They seldom make us."

Perkins's reputation was spreading. On March 12, 1927, a glowing article appeared in the *Manchester Guardian,* a prestigious weekly newspaper published in England. After observing Perkins in action, the British reporter wrote, "I have met a considerable number and wide range of interesting women in the United States, but none who has impressed me more than this squarely-built woman with her shrewd, alert face, keen, wide-apart eyes, and warmly human personality. . . . She has won every inch of her way to the high office she now holds by service, efficiency, and a remarkable combination of courage and humour."

The reporter was particularly impressed with how Perkins handled workmen's compensation appeal cases and wrote, "The people never become mere 'cases' to her. . . . I never sat under a judge who was better at getting at the facts, nor swifter in apprehension of their relevance."

In one compensation case, the insurance company was fighting against paying insurance money to a construction worker who had been hit on the head with a heavy bucket. Since his injury, the man hadn't been able to work because he had episodes of weird and wild behavior. The insurance company said that the man had been a "constitutional mental inferior" *before* the accident. As proof, the insurance company's lawyer introduced evidence that the man had gotten poor marks in the fourth grade. Perkins listened to both sides and ordered the insurance company to compensate the man.

The insurance company was slow to pay, and the confused man thought it was Perkins's fault. So, he came to her office with a knife. When he couldn't find her, he rushed into the hall and cut the throat of the first person he met. Ironically, it was the lawyer for the insurance company. Just then Perkins appeared.

"I stepped out of the washroom, and what did I see, but a man with a knife in his hand and Mr. Geddings bleeding from the throat," Perkins recalled. The man ran off and Perkins held the wounded lawyer until the police arrived. The man was arrested and committed to a mental hospital. Perkins made sure his family got the compensation money.

In 1928, Governor Al Smith ran for president of the United

States. He was the first Roman Catholic candidate in American history, and a variety of bigoted individuals and groups, including the Ku Klux Klan, campaigned against Smith. They were very nasty. Undaunted, Perkins traveled to eleven states to campaign for Smith. In some places, she was booed and pelted with eggs and rotten tomatoes. But she did not quit. With her ever-ready sense of humor, Perkins complimented a group of hecklers on their aim when their tomatoes hit her on her skirt and her foot.

In September, Perkins delivered a speech over the radio in support of Smith. "Now the test has come, as never before, since we had the suffrage—the test of the power and loyalty and intelligence of women voters," Perkins said.

But the smear campaign was too effective, and Smith lost the election to Herbert Hoover. Although disappointed, Perkins was not surprised. And she was pleased that Franklin Delano Roosevelt was elected governor of New York State. Since her disappointment with Roosevelt during the fight for the fifty-four-hour bill, Perkins had come to know him better and respect him, particularly after he survived a severe bout of polio in 1921. Although both his legs were left paralyzed, Roosevelt refused to limit his life. Perkins greatly admired his courage and determination to return to politics. Smith and Roosevelt were both Democrats and friends, and Smith told Perkins that he had encouraged Roosevelt to keep her on as chair of the Industrial Board.

Roosevelt, however, had a bigger idea. He wanted Perkins to be the industrial commissioner, or the head of the entire New York State Department of Labor. As industrial commissioner, Perkins would become a member of the governor's cabinet, the first woman cabinet member in New York.

CHAPTER FIVE

Working Together

1929–1932

"... the beauty of loyalty and chivalry between women."

Before appointing Perkins industrial commissioner, Governor-elect Roosevelt asked Governor Al Smith what he thought about the idea.

"Well, you should give it a lot of thought. When she is commissioner she will have charge of administering the whole Department of Labor—all the men who work as factory inspectors and on the compensation boards. I have always thought that, as a rule, men will take advice from a woman, but it is hard for them to take orders from a woman," Smith replied.

Roosevelt repeated Smith's comments to Perkins. "I've got more nerve about women and their status in the world than Al has," he said with a chuckle.

Although Perkins laughed, too, she could not "resist the temptation to say, 'But it was more of a victory for Al to bring himself to appoint a woman, never appointed before, when I was unknown, than it is for you when I have a record as a responsible public officer for almost ten years.' "

Perkins was confirmed without fuss. In fact, her appointment was applauded by organized labor and manufacturers. She was sworn in on January 14, 1929. Her daughter, Susanna, now twelve years old, and a large group of friends, including Rose Schneiderman, attended the ceremony.

On January 31, more than eight hundred people gathered to honor Perkins at an elegant luncheon at the Hotel Astor in New York City. Labor and business leaders gave speeches. Then Perkins spoke. "I take it that we are gathered not so much to celebrate Frances Perkins, the person, as we are to celebrate Frances Perkins as the symbol of an idea. It is an idea that has been at work among us for many years—the idea that social justice is possible in a great industrial community," she said.

Frances Perkins promised the audience that she would do three things:

On January 14, 1929, Perkins was sworn in as New York State industrial commissioner. She and Susanna, twelve, pose here for newspaper photographers. The flowers are from friends and supporters. (UPI/BETTMANN)

I promise to use the brains I have to meet problems with intelligence and courage.

I promise that I will be candid about what I know, of the Labor Department or of the state of industry in this state and in this country.

I promise to all of you who have a right to know, the whole truth and nothing but the truth, so far as I can speak it. If I have been wrong, you may tell me so, for I really have no pride in judgment. I know that all judgment is relative. It may be right today and wrong tomorrow. The only thing that can make it truly right is the desire to have it constantly moving in the right direction.

Perkins always felt that she was "the product" of all the people throughout her life who contributed "to my knowledge, to my information, and to my character." During her luncheon speech, she thanked them: the "engineers, architects, chemists, physicists, men, who . . . taught me in private lessons, for nothing, what makes a safe factory"; her coworkers at the Labor Department; her household help, "the women who have helped me bring up my child and take care of my home"; her husband "who has put a brilliant mind to work on some of my knotty problems"; her "good daughter"; and the "loyal, intelligent, and wise women of New York." In particular she thanked "that mother of us all," Florence Kelley. "Countless times, Mrs. Kelley's steely look and steady, 'Frances, you've got to do it!' have meant the difference between doing it that year and not doing it at all."

Mary (Molly) W. Dewson, president of the New York State Consumers' League, had arranged the luncheon. "Dear Molly," Perkins wrote to her afterward, "I cannot tell you how much that luncheon which you arranged for me has meant in my life and I want you to know not only that I am grateful for all that you did to make it a success, but that it has given me a new insight into the beauty of loyalty and chivalry between women. How fine it is to play the game together all these years, isn't it?"

A close associate of Florence Kelley, Dewson was an experienced social reformer and political activist. A tall, self-confident woman, she was passionately committed to getting legislation passed that promoted social justice. As she saw how women like Perkins successfully educated and motivated male politicians, Dewson became committed to getting more women involved in politics and government. Perkins and Dewson had never become personal friends, but they had collaborated for years. "I conferred with her constantly on legislation, not only with regard to wages but with regard to the hours of labor for women, child labor legislation, Workmen's Compensation . . . and other such matters," Perkins said.

Perkins had been reluctant to accept Roosevelt's appointment because she felt that although being chair of the Industrial Board was "the perfect job . . . fascinating and gave one all the authority one wanted. I was not anxious to be the Industrial Commissioner. That office, I knew, had all the problems and complications of administration," she later recalled. "However, it seemed the right thing to do. I had been taught long ago by my grandmother that if anybody opens a door, one should always go through. Opportunity comes that way."

It was only after Roosevelt assured her that he would support her efforts to propose legislation to reduce working hours, improve workmen's compensation, restrict child labor, abolish sweatshops, and establish more safety codes that Perkins agreed to the appointment. "When you need help, come to me and I will do everything I can. I am for the program—all of it. Keep me posted so I won't make mistakes when I don't know exactly what is going on," Roosevelt told her.

Roosevelt kept his word and supported Perkins's various programs. He valued her opinions, respected her judgment, and relied on her for information and advice. During this time, Perkins developed a close working relationship with Roosevelt. "You study the person you are working for; you study them not out of curiosity, but in order to appreciate their mentality, their purpose, the best side of their nature, and their weaknesses, so that you may work with them and accomplish with them and for them the thing which they really desire and hope to accomplish," Perkins once said.

Perkins soon realized that Roosevelt understood a problem better if she described it "in human terms." So, she always made sure she included vivid descriptions in addition to her statistics and chart including stories about the men who got silicosis, a serious lung disease, from polishing the inside of glass milk tanks; about the girls who got radium poisoning because they used their lips to wet the fine hair brushes into a point when they painted luminous dials on the clock faces; about the old carpenter who lost his arm and was cheated out of about five thousand dollars because he didn't get a hearing for his compensation case; and about the dirt and disorder she found in the Public Employment Service office, a free state employment agency that was supposed to help people find jobs.

In January 1929, when Roosevelt became governor and Perkins took office, the New York State Department of Labor had seventeen hundred employees and branch offices in seven cities. Perkins's annual salary was twelve thousand dollars, a good salary at that time. She divided her time between the department headquarters in Albany and the branch office in New York City, where she lived in an apartment with Susanna and Paul, who was in an "up" phase of his "up and down illness."

An intense and energetic person, Perkins required very

little sleep (except in August, when she and her family spent the month at the Brick House in Maine—then Perkins spent most of the first two weeks in bed). She would need every bit of her energy to cope with the crisis that was about to overcome New York and the nation.

In 1929, the American economy appeared to be thriving. There were 20 million telephones in America, twice as many as in the rest of the world combined. Phones with a mouthpiece and receiver were beginning to appear, but most were wooden boxes on the wall with a crank to ring up an operator or a stand-up phone with a hook to hold the receiver. *Business Week* magazine began publication. People were buying stocks, or shares in companies, in record numbers.

But as Perkins studied employment statistics, she noticed something else going on—"it was evident to those of us who watched industry closely that there was great irregularity in employment." The great irregularity was a sign of economic troubles that had been brewing since World War I ended in 1918.

Part of the trouble was that American factories started producing vast numbers of consumer goods—automobiles, refrigerators, stoves, and radios. But wages were too low for people to buy all of the consumer goods being produced. When people did buy, they frequently bought on credit. "Buy now, pay later!" they were told. And they did, going deeper and deeper into debt.

Finally, people stopped buying. Goods piled up. Factories stopped producing so many goods and workers lost their jobs. Prices fell. Companies were not making money and investors, who had been buying like crazy, started to sell their shares. On October 24, 1929, 13 million shares of stock were sold. The value of stocks fell below the price people had paid for them. Panic spread. Values continued to drop. Five days later, October 29, more than 16 million shares were sold off. Unlike today there were no regulations or safeguards to control the situation. "In a few short weeks it had blown into thin air *thirty billion dollars* . . . ," one newspaper reporter wrote.

President Herbert Hoover kept insisting that the situation would get better, that the worst was over. But it wasn't. Thousands of banks closed. Unable to get their money, businesses closed. People lost their jobs. The businesses that stayed open lowered their wages, lower and lower.

In New York State, Perkins and Roosevelt started studying ways to put people back to work. Perkins also developed more accurate ways to collect information about the employment situation.

On January 21, 1930, on her way to work, Perkins read in a front-page article in the *New York Times* that Hoover had announced that employment had improved and that things were much better. "As I read and realized that this came from the President of the United States, I was horrified, for I knew that he had been grossly misinformed. . . . As I read the story over again I became more indignant, because I knew it was going to hurt and grieve the people being laid off in great numbers. . . . They would feel there was something wrong with them personally if the President said that the employment situation was better the country over. A great despair would enter their hearts and they would say, 'Why don't I get a job if things are better?' " Perkins said.

Perkins felt that it was her "duty to make a correction." She spent a whole day gathering accurate data. The next day she held a press conference and "issued a statement that the President was wrong. . . . Unemployment was increasing . . . things were worse." She "felt the satisfaction of one who has told the truth."

Much to Perkins's astonishment, she discovered that

she had caused a great furor for challenging the president of the United States. Years later Perkins said, "I know now that I had no proper perspective on the prestige and position of the President of the United States. He seemed to me just another citizen, and I thought that if he was wrong, it was my duty to make a correction since I had access to true information."

Perkins's statement made the front page of newspapers. She was besieged with telegrams and telephone calls. Some people applauded her. Others condemned her. Roosevelt called to say, "Bully for you! That was a fine statement and I am glad you made it." Perkins apologized for not consulting with him in advance. "Well, I think it was better you didn't. If you had asked me, I would probably have told you not to do it, and I think it is much more wholesome to have it right out in the open," Roosevelt responded.

Perkins encouraged Roosevelt to appoint a committee to study how to stabilize employment.

"In 1930 the governor agreed with me that we ought to make an attempt to educate the people as well as ourselves about the things that could be done, not only to relieve this crisis, but to prevent unemployment in the future, or at least to mitigate its drastic effect upon those who could least bear the burden," Perkins recalled.

In March Roosevelt appointed the Committee on Stabilization of Industry for the Prevention of Unemployment, and New York became the first state to study formally the problem of unemployment. The committee held hearings throughout the state, consulted with experts, and concluded that unemployment "is just as much of an industrial hazard as accidents, and should therefore be insured in advance."

The idea of unemployment insurance was a new idea in the United States. Other industrialized countries like England

Perkins organized the National Governors' Conference on Unemployment in January 1931. She is pictured here with two leading businessmen: Max Meyer (left) *of New York City and Maxwell Wheeler* (right) *of Buffalo.* (U.S. DEPARTMENT OF LABOR)

had some type of unemployment insurance, but not the U.S. Perkins had been supporting the idea for years. She worked hard to educate other people about the need for such insurance. Finally, at the 1931 National Governors' Conference in Salt Lake City, Roosevelt became the first major political figure in America to endorse the idea of unemployment insurance. In the summer of 1931, Roosevelt asked Perkins to go to England to study their system of unemployment insurance. Taking Susanna with her, Perkins traveled by ship to England, where she conducted her usual thorough investigation.

Perkins returned to a whirlwind of activity. Based on her research, she wrote an article about her ideas for "an American plan" of unemployment insurance. She also continued pushing for legislation to protect women and children workers and for ways to solve unemployment. Perkins gave countless numbers of speeches and testified before committees in Washington and Albany. She streamlined the state employment agency in New York and lobbied for a federal employment service. She organized a major conference where Roosevelt met with the governors of Connecticut, Maine, Massachusetts, New Hampshire, New Jersey, Ohio, and Pennsylvania to find ways to deal with the crisis. All the while, Hoover insisted that the worst of the depression was over.

But it wasn't; it was getting worse.

On February 17, 1932, Perkins's mentor, Florence Kelley, died. Perkins spoke at her funeral. "There are many women in this audience today, whose first knowledge of Florence Kelley came when they were young women in college or in school. . . . She took a whole group of young people, formless in their aspirations, and molded their aspirations for social justice into some definite purpose. . . ." Kelley was buried in Maine. Carved on Kelley's headstone were the words, "She made everyone brave."

That same year Roosevelt became the Democratic candidate for president and promised "a new deal for the American people." The unemployment figure had soared to a record high. Wages declined to about 60 percent less than they were the year before. Industry operated at half the capacity it had the year before. And an "army," the Bonus Army, made up of World War I veterans and their families, built a camp in Washington, D.C. Unemployed, hungry people without homes, jobs, food, or decent clothes, the veterans had come to ask Congress to pay them a "bonus" they had been promised. But Congress refused. Hoover ordered an infantry, cavalry, and tank corp of the United States Army to disband the Bonus Army. And they did, with tear gas, bayonets, horses, and tanks. Two veterans were killed and a baby was crushed to death.

On November 8, 1932, Roosevelt was elected in a landslide victory over Herbert Hoover. "The election in the Fall of 1932 . . . was a vote against the depression—a bewildered people, viewing the chaos in which their lives were staged, voted overwhelmingly for what they called a 'New Deal.' " Perkins wrote.

Rumors started circulating that Roosevelt was going to appoint Perkins to his cabinet. Perkins denied the rumors. And she informed Roosevelt that her "opinion is against the idea." But Roosevelt had another idea. So did Molly Dewson.

CHAPTER SIX

Madam Secretary

1933

"It is there to be done, so I do it."

Even before Roosevelt was elected, Dewson had been lobbying for Perkins's appointment. She arranged for newspaper and magazine articles about Perkins. She invited Perkins to speak at important conferences. And she made sure Roosevelt was inundated with letters from influential people. Dewson's goal was to "make it an endless chain" of letters supporting Perkins.

The possibility of Perkins's appointment was widely discussed. On January 5, 1933, the *Boston Post* published an article, "Boston Girl First Woman Cabinet Member?" The caption under her photograph read, "What will Frances Perkins, Boston-born and Massachusetts-educated woman, do now that her boss, Franklin D. Roosevelt, is to be President? It is rumored that she may be the next Secretary of Labor—thereby making her the first woman ever to sit in the Cabinet." There was also widespread support from leading citizens and influential newspapers and magazines. Jane Addams, the founder of Hull House who had recently been awarded the Nobel Peace Prize, endorsed her. An article appeared in *McCall's Magazine* in which the writer concluded that Perkins was a "logical choice" because "she is a leader. . . . American labor today knows that it needs more than an administrator and a megaphone. It needs a Pillar of Fire."

When Perkins expressed her reluctance, Dewson said, "Don't be such a baby, Frances. You do the right thing. I'll murder you if you don't."

But Perkins wasn't being "a baby." She had serious reasons for not wanting to become the secretary of labor. First of all, she "was not a bona fide labor person." Previous labor secretaries had been union men. And, as Perkins told Roosevelt, "labor had always had, and would expect to have, one of its own people as Secretary." In addition, she would have to move to Washington, D.C., and that would present her with "many grave personal difficulties." It would not be easy to disrupt Paul, who was in a "down" phase of his illness, or Susanna, a teenager who was settled into her life in New York City. There were also the financial pressures Perkins faced; Paul's various hospitalizations were expensive. Perkins had been offered jobs in private industry that paid a lot more money than government jobs.

On February 22, 1933, Roosevelt invited Perkins to his house at East Sixty-fifth Street in New York City. That was the same year Adolf Hitler took control of Germany and established concentration camps for internment of political "undesirables." Forty-two black Americans were lynched in the South. Prohibition against the sale of alcohol in America ended with ratification of the Twenty-first Amendment. The typical yearly salary for a public school teacher was $1,227, a lawyer $4,218, a doctor $3,382, a sleep-in household helper $260. Gasoline cost eighteen cents a gallon, eggs twenty-one cents a dozen, and milk ten cents a quart. Phillip Morris cigarettes were introduced in America. So was Windex, for cleaning windows, Ritz Crackers,

Campbell's Chicken Noodle Soup, and Dy-Dee-Doll, a doll that sucked water from a bottle and wet its diapers. Helen Jacobs won the women's single-tennis championship at Wimbledon. She wore shorts, the other women players wore skirts knee-length or longer.

"My appointment was for eight, but I arrived early," Perkins recalled. "The place was a shambles. . . . The constant flow of visitors left the small staff of servants powerless to retain any semblance of order. Furniture was broken. Rugs were rolled up and piled in a corner. Overshoes and muddy rubbers were in a heap near the door. The floor was littered with newspapers. . . ."

Roosevelt wasted no time telling Perkins that he wanted her to be secretary of labor.

She tried to talk him out of it. But it was no use. Finally she tried another approach. "I said that if I accepted the position of Secretary of Labor I should want to do a great deal," Perkins recalled. Then she outlined an extensive program of "labor legislation and economic improvements." Her plan included a federal law of minimum wages, maximum hours, unemployment and old-age insurance, the end of child labor, the creation of a federal employment service, immediate aid to the states for direct unemployment relief, and health insurance.

"Are you sure you want these things done? Because you don't want me for Secretary of Labor if you don't," Perkins concluded.

"Yes, I'll back you," Roosevelt answered.

Finally, Perkins agreed to become secretary of labor. "The overwhelming argument and thought which made me do it in the end in spite of personal difficulties was the realization that the door might not be opened to a woman again for a long, long time, and that I had a kind of duty to other women to walk in and sit down on the chair that was offered, and so establish the right of others long hence and far-distant in geography to sit in the high seat," Perkins later explained.

Perkins went to talk with her husband, Paul, who was in a hospital, because she would "never dream of doing a thing that he hadn't been informed of and consulted about in advance."

"I can't go to Washington. I will not go to Washington! Where will I live?" he responded. Perkins suggested that they keep their New York apartment. Susanna would continue to live there with a live-in housekeeper. Paul, too, when he was well enough. Perkins would come home every weekend.

"You promise you'll be up every weekend? You'll come up and see me every weekend?" Paul asked.

Perkins promised.

On February 28, 1933, Franklin Roosevelt announced his appointment of Frances Perkins as secretary of labor.

Many organizations and individuals applauded Roosevelt's decision. "When I think of Frances Perkins's point of view and attitude, her humanity, wisdom and statesmanship, it seems to me that she will be an angel at the Cabinet table . . . ," wrote Oswald Garrison Villard, editor of the *Nation*. But as Perkins had predicted, organized labor opposed her appointment. "Labor can never become reconciled to the selection made," announced William Green, president of the American Federation of Labor. "We simply will not deal with the lady, that is all," said another labor spokesman.

Before she left New York for Washington, Perkins agreed to meet with a group of reporters. When asked about organized labor's reaction, Perkins said that they were "within their rights in taking that position. What is more, I am glad the whole thing is open and above-board. It is infinitely more wholesome. On the other hand, to say that they will not be reconciled is one thing and to say that they will not cooperate is another. I have not the slightest doubt that I may expect the fullest cooperation. Mr. Green is an old friend of mine, and he is a man of great patriotism."

When the reporters asked about her personal life, Perkins, as usual, bristled. "Is that quite necessary?" she replied. Later she explained. "We New Englanders keep ourselves to ourselves."

Reluctantly Perkins did give the reporters some personal information: she didn't own a radio; she planned to continue signing her paychecks as Frances Perkins; she no longer played tennis, just a little golf; and she maintained her lifelong interest in art, particularly modern art and the paintings of Diego Rivera and Georgia O'Keeffe.

As usual, a reporter commented on Perkins's eyes describing them as "shining even more than usual." On another occasion, a reporter, Genevieve Parkhurst, wrote, "But it is her eyes that tell her story. Large and dark and vivid, they take their expression from her mood. If she is amused they scintillate with little points of light. If moved to sympathy or compassion they cloud over. At the slightest suspicion of insincerity or injustice they can become keen and searching."

Mary Harriman Rumsey, an activist and close friend of Perkins's, suggested that they share a house in Washington. Perkins, whose finances were stretched very thin, was grateful. Rumsey found a small octagon house, a house with eight sides, in the Georgetown section of Washington. She furnished it and paid for a staff of household workers. Perkins insisted on paying her share of other expenses.

As the first woman cabinet member, Perkins faced an unexpected problem. People did not know how to address her. Was she Miss Secretary or Mrs. Secretary. Or what? "Why not, 'Madame Secretary,' if that form is to be used at all? One is accustomed to 'madam chairman' or 'madam president', so it comes more naturally, don't you think?" Perkins suggested to one person who had gotten tongue-tied. A newspaper reporter overheard the conversation and wrote an article that appeared in the *New York Times* with the headline, " 'Madam Secretary' Miss Perkins's Choice." And so, that became her title. (Except for some people who did not like her ideas and privately referred to her as "That Woman!")

The Department of Labor was supposed "to foster, promote, and develop the welfare of the wage earners of the United States, to improve their working conditions, and to advance their opportunities for profitable employment." But with the exception of the Children's Bureau, headed by Grace Abbott, and the Women's Bureau, headed by Mary Anderson, the Department of Labor was not carrying out its mission. "The offices were dirty, files and papers were missing, there was no program or plan of work, there was an internal spy system, and everyone was scared of everyone else and trying to get into my good graces," Perkins wrote later.

Without delay, Perkins got to work to get the department fully functioning. For starters, she abolished the two different lunchrooms, one for black and one for white workers. Although segregated facilities were the norm in Washington and the rest of the country, Perkins was not going to allow them.

Just weeks after she took office, Perkins held a press conference. "Miss Perkins Wields Her Broom Vigorously in Labor Department," one newspaper headline read. "Firm of voice and emphatic in her gestures, the first woman cabinet member told newspapermen today the present establishment is not to her liking and that she intends to take it virtually apart and remake it," a reporter wrote.

Perkins announced that she had disbanded a "secret service" squad set up by William Doak, her predecessor. Part of Doak's campaign to rid America of "unwanted foreigners" and

President Franklin Roosevelt with his cabinet during his second administration. Perkins sat at the end because the Department of Labor was created after the other departments. Roosevelt is at the front end of the table. The signatures, from left to right and top to bottom, are: Franklin D. Roosevelt, Homer Cummings, Claude A. Swanson, Jhn. [John] N. Garner, Daniel C. Roper, Henry Morgenthau, Jr., Frances Perkins, Harold L. Ickes, Cordell Hull, Henry A. Wallace, Harry H. Woodring, and James A. Farley. (FRANKLIN DELANO ROOSEVELT LIBRARY)

to "keep American jobs for Americans," the squad operated out of the Bureau of Immigration. Before she arrived in Washington, Perkins had heard rumors about the squad's illegal, strong-armed efforts to deport aliens, or foreign-born persons who weren't American citizens. Quickly discovering that the rumors were true, Perkins disbanded the "secret squad" and appointed Daniel MacCormack as head of the Bureau of Immigration. "We realized that we held tremendous power over the lives and freedom of human beings and we tried not to use our power arbitrarily," she said.

Determined to provide statistical information that the person "on the street can understand," Perkins also announced the reorganization of the Bureau of Labor Statistics. She hired an expert economist, Isador Lubin, to head the bureau. Soon the bureau was producing accurate, practical information about employment, living costs, prices, wages, and other aspects of the economy—the kind of information Perkins believed people needed in order to make intelligent decisions, policies, and programs.

Finally, Perkins told reporters that she had reorganized the employment service and created a nationwide system of free employment agencies, soon known as the United States Employment Service, where jobless people could seek assistance in finding jobs. This had been one of the programs Perkins presented to Roosevelt before she agreed to become secretary of labor. Within four years, 19 million people would find jobs through this employment service.

The depression was much harder on black workers than white. Segregation and racism were a way of life in America and unemployment for black workers was 30 to 60 percent greater than for white workers. Perkins made a special effort to improve the situation. She prohibited the Employment Service from discriminating against job seekers. She hired Lawrence Oxley as a special assistant in charge of the newly created Division of Negro Labor. Years later, Oxley, the first African-American man to hold an executive position in the Department of Labor, recalled Perkins welcoming him with a handshake and the words, "Mr. Oxley, we are awfully glad to have you join our family."

On March 24, 1933, fifteen hundred people gathered to honor Perkins at a formal dinner at the Hotel Commodore in New York City. After nine prominent people gave speeches praising her, Perkins spoke. As usual, she reiterated her unshakable belief in social justice. She also said that she was happy that her "beloved daughter" was there to hear her flattered because "it has always been a matter of negotiation between us as to whether or not she should override my decisions. . . ."

Perkins ended her speech by thanking two groups of people who weren't there. First, ". . . the whole procession of all the women who have tried during these hundreds of years, the women who made life better for women . . . who have opened doors for us . . . ," Perkins said. "I want to be worthy of them."

Then Perkins thanked the workers, the "men and women who have no work, no wages and very little to eat," and all the workers she had met as an investigator and commissioner. "They, too, are my friends and many of them have taught me about life and have told me of things I would not have known without their cooperation and their sympathy and good will," Perkins said.

Before attending her first official cabinet meeting, Perkins was "apprehensive and on guard." Mostly she was worried that the men might think that she "was too talkative." Perkins sat quietly until Roosevelt said, "Frances, don't you want to say something?"

"I didn't want to, but I knew I had to," Perkins later wrote. "There was silence. My colleagues [who Perkins later noted were also "quite still and solemn and uncertain"] looked at me with tense curiosity. I think some weren't sure I could speak.

"I said what I had to say, quickly and briefly. I had called a conference of labor leaders and experts to draft recommendations for relief of unemployment. I said a program of public works should be one of the first steps."

The need for action was critical. "Banks were collapsing throughout the nation. Relief stations were closing down for lack of funds. Hunger marchers were on parade. Food riots were becoming more common. Crime, born of the need for food, clothing, and other necessities of life, was on the upsurge," Perkins later wrote.

The first woman cabinet member Frances Perkins had achieved her historic first at a time when the American people, particularly the workers, were desperate. Unafraid, Perkins was determined to deal with the crisis. "It is there to be done, so I do it . . . ," she once said.

CHAPTER SEVEN

The New Deal and Bloody Thursday

1933–1938

"We were always in a crisis."

*F*rances Perkins was in the thick of the action as Roosevelt launched his New Deal. She reviewed thousands of ideas. Met with experts. Proposed programs. Revised programs. Over and over again, she testified before Congress about various measures. Within the span of "One Hundred Days," Congress passed a slew of proposals aimed at ending the Great Depression.

Perkins was intimately involved in developing many of the measures, including the Civilian Conservation Corp (CCC). One of Roosevelt's favorite projects, the CCC offered young men food, clothing, medical care, and a dollar a day to work at jobs that improved national parks and forests. Living in camps, CCC workers built wildlife shelters, dug canals, restored historic battlefields, stocked rivers and lakes with nearly a billion fish, cleared beaches and campgrounds, and planted trees—2 billion trees by 1941. Although the CCC ended in 1941, plaques acknowledging the workers can still be found in many national parks and forests.

Although on a much smaller scale, CCC camps for unemployed young women were also set up (8,500 women bene-fitted compared to 2.5 million men). The first one, a racially integrated camp eventually named Camp Jane Addams, was set up in Bear Mountain Park in New York. Since at that time physical labor was considered too manly for women to do, CCC camps were set up to teach unemployed women a variety of skills, including homemaking and personal hygiene. Of course, women today would not stand for such treatment, but, in 1933, even the idea of CCC camps for women was bold. Without the support of Eleanor Roosevelt, who called a White House Conference on Camps for Unemployed Women, and Frances Perkins, nothing would have happened.

Perkins was also involved in the development of the Federal Emergency Relief Administration (FERA), a program that gave matching grants to the states to provide food, clothing, fuel, medicine, housing, and other necessities for unemployed people. According to Perkins, FERA was the "first step in the economic pump priming to break the back of the depression."

In the last days of the "One Hundred Days," Congress passed Roosevelt's most ambitious and important piece of legislation, the National Industrial Recovery Act (NIRA). Perkins worked long hours with other advisers in drafting the legislation. "We counted greatly on NIRA to act as a shot in the arm for industry...," Perkins wrote.

NIRA contained a substantial federal public works program, the Public Works Administration (PWA). When the government created a job for an unemployed worker, the worker in turn could pay the grocer, the grocer in turn could pay the farmer, the farmer could buy supplies like a tractor that a factory produced. "With one dollar paid for relief or public works or anything else, you have created four dollars worth of national income," Perkins pointed out.

The PWA spent 6 billion dollars and put people to work

on various projects, including building low-cost housing, airports, the Triborough Bridge in New York City, the Grand Coulee Dam on the Columbia River near Spokane, Washington, and almost three-quarters of America's new schools. "It is my opinion that the principal factor in our economic recovery was the expenditure of public funds for public works," Perkins wrote later.

NIRA also set up the National Recovery Administration (NRA), an agency with the responsibility of stabilizing wages and prices and reviving production. To do this, NRA had the authority to work with industries and workers to develop codes, or guidelines, that set standards for wages, prices, working conditions, production, marketing practices, and other issues. The codes were voluntary. Three different advisory boards were created to help develop them. Perkins named Rose Schneiderman as a member of the Labor Advisory Board.

Business leaders were pleased because the codes were exempt, or free, from existing antitrust laws, or laws that prevented industries from engaging in such business practices as price fixing or forming huge combinations. Labor leaders were pleased because in addition to defining maximum hours, minimum wages, and safe working conditions, the codes gave workers the right to organize, or to form unions.

The NRA was launched with a massive publicity campaign featuring a motto, "We Do Our Part," and a symbol, the Blue Eagle, a fierce-looking blue bird that looked like a cross between the American eagle and the Indian thunderbird. Consumers were urged to deal with businesses that adopted codes and displayed the Blue Eagle. Rallies and parades were held. By September 1933, most major industries had developed codes.

"The NRA was enormously popular. The Blue Eagle spread everywhere ... there was a great lift in the spirit of the

*Perkins at the first meeting of the National Recovery Administration (NRA) in 1933. General Hugh S. Johnson, head of the NRA, is seated to her left. The other people were advisers. From left to right, back to front: Joseph Franklin, president of the International Boilermakers Union; John Frey of the Metals Trade Department, American Federation of Labor (AFL); Edward F. McGrady, former legislative representative of the AFL; Sidney Hillman, president of the Amalgamated Clothing Workers; Rose Schneiderman, secretary of the Women's Trade Union League; Perkins; Johnson; Dr. Leo Wolman, economist; and John L. Lewis, president of the United Mine Workers. (*TAMIMENT INSTITUTE LIBRARY, NEW YORK UNIVERSITY*)*

people as they marched in parades, proudly displayed the Blue Eagle in their windows . . . they began to have faith in themselves, and they determined to make it work," Perkins wrote later.

The steel industry developed one of the first codes. Frances Perkins represented the interests of the steel workers. Determined to let the steel workers know that she was "realistically and vigorously" considering their needs, Perkins decided to visit some steel factories. She informed Roosevelt about her decision.

"That's a good idea. But don't get yourself arrested," Roosevelt said.

Not wanting to descend with an official entourage, Perkins considered going alone. Then she decided to take Father Francis Haas with her. "I chose him because he was a friend of labor, because the cloth of his profession, I felt, would give us standing, and because I needed at least one other individual to go along as aide and observer and helper. I did not want to go 'in state' with a battery of economic advisers, publicity men, minor public officials, and obsequious secretaries." Later Perkins was criticized for not taking an entourage. Never mind, Roosevelt told her. "You and I have the instinct for freedom of association," he said. "Unfortunately, I can't practice it any more. What with the Secret Service and the politicians ... But keep it up as long as you can, don't let them get you down. The common people don't care about all that style, Frances, and, after all, you and I are engaged in trying to bring them into things."

Perkins toured steel factories in western Pennsylvania. "To go through a great steel plant is a thrilling experience. There is no such blazing light in Fourth of July fireworks as when they tip the great containers and let out the white-hot steel; there are no more beautiful colors than the violet and rose tones that steel takes on as it cools—and perhaps no more strenuous place to work than at the open-hearth furnaces where steel is made," Perkins later wrote.

Everywhere she went she asked questions: "What were the hours? What were the wages? What constituted a week of employment and how much employment was there in a year? How about accident insurance and unemployment insurance, and did they carry pensions for the workers? What about age limits? What was the present accident rate? And what were the safety devices to keep it down?"

She ate lunch in the cafeteria with the workers. She visited them in their homes. In Homestead, Pennsylvania, the site of a bitter and bloody labor dispute in 1892, she arranged with the burgess, or mayor, to hold a meeting in the Hall of Burgesses. As the meeting ended, she heard a disturbance downstairs. "A newspaperman whispered that a lot of men were in the lower hall and on the sidewalk because the Burgess had not allowed them to come in," Perkins wrote later.

Perkins asked to meet with the men.

According to Perkins, "The Burgess, red in the face, puffed and stormed. 'No, no you've had enough. These men are not any good. They're undesirable Reds. . . . They just want to make trouble.'"

Unafraid, Perkins insisted on talking with them. "I had been brought up in the tradition of free speech. I took it for granted that it was the 'duty of public officers,' as Plato says, 'to listen patiently to all citizens,'" she later explained.

Perkins went outside and started to speak with the crowd.

The burgess appeared with the police in tow. "You can't talk here . . . there is a rule against making a speech here," he shouted.

"All right—I am sorry. We will go over to the public park," Perkins said.

"You can't do that, there is an ordinance against holding meetings in a public park," the red-faced burgess shouted.

Perkins protested. Then she spotted the American flag flying over a building and realized that it must be the post office. As an officer of the federal government, Perkins figured that she "must have some rights there."

"We will go to the post office, there is the American flag," she told the crowd.

The post office was about to close. Quickly Perkins explained the situation. The postmaster let her and the crowd in. "We stood in the long corridor lined with postal cages. Somebody got me a chair, and I stood on it and made a brief speech about the steel code. I asked if anybody wanted to speak," she wrote later. About thirty men did. Perkins listened and invited the "most vocal and obstreperous of the speakers" to testify at a public hearing in Washington.

A local newspaper reporter wrote about the incident and wired the story to the national news. By the time Perkins returned to Washington, the press was waiting for her. They asked her why the burgess behaved the way he did. "Why, he seemed a little nervous," Perkins replied.

"You did just the right thing . . . ," Roosevelt told her as he laughed at Perkins's description about the "nervous Burgess of Homestead."

Within weeks, the steel code was completed and specified minimum wages, maximum hours, abolition of child labor, and safe, sanitary working conditions. "The code as it was finally adopted was not a perfect code," Perkins wrote later. "It left much to be desired, but at least it opened the door to a continuing improvement in the lives, the work and wages of the people who work in steel." A door that Perkins had devoted her life to opening.

Perkins also supported collective bargaining, or the right of workers to organize unions and negotiate with owners for better wages, hours, and working conditions. Under Section 7 (a) of the NIRA, workers were given the legal right to form unions and bargain collectively.

Workers had been forming unions for years. In fact, as early as 1794, a group of shoemakers in Philadelphia formed the Federal Society of Journeymen Cordwainers. And workers had been protesting unfair conditions by going on strike, or refusing to work. The first recorded strike happened in 1768, when New York tailors refused to work because their wages had been lowered.

At first, unions were made up of skilled craftsmen. But as industries with factories spread across America, factory workers and unskilled laborers formed unions. By the 1820s and 1830s, unions started not only to fight to get better benefits for workers but also to elect people to public office who would pass laws to reform conditions.

In 1881 in Columbus, Ohio, a group of trade unions joined together to form the American Federation of Labor (AFL). It grew to be a very important national union organization.

As unions became more powerful, employers worked hard to undermine them. They used such methods as getting the court to issue an injunction, or an order that forced striking union members to return to work or find another job. Some employers would not hire workers unless they agreed not to join a union. They also hired scabs, or workers who were willing to do striking workers' jobs. Union members were fired and harassed.

Time and time again violence broke out. There were gun battles and fistfights. In April 1886 in East St. Louis, Missouri, seven workers were killed in a battle between strikers and the police. After the workers burned down a railroad freight depot, the governor called in seven hundred National Guardsmen. In July 1892 in Coeur d'Alene, Idaho, six hundred strikers were arrested and confined in bull pens.

In 1914, Congress passed the Clayton Anti-Trust Act, which limited the use of injunctions and said that unions had the right to exist. By 1919, the AFL had over 4 million members. But by 1933, it had less than 2 million members. During a depression, workers who had jobs did not dare risk joining a union.

But Section 7 (a) of the NIRA changed that by making it legal for unions to organize. And, for the first time, employers were required to deal with unions. Labor leaders rushed to organize workers, and the newly organized workers started to make demands. But employers found ways to ignore them. A series of strikes swept the nation. Some were violent. "50 Are Shot in Minneapolis As Police Fire on Strikers; Gas Routs Seattle Pickets" read a front-page newspaper headline on July 21, 1934. On September 6, 1934, there were front-page newspaper headlines about a textile strike in Trion, Georgia: ". . . 24 Shot in Riots at Mills," and a textile strike in Charlotte, North Carolina: "Troops Called Out in North Carolina."

"Almost the entire period of the Roosevelt administration was marked by difficulties in normal relationships between workers and employers . . . we were always in a crisis," Perkins later wrote.

One of the most "ticklish" crises Perkins handled was the longshoremen's strike in San Francisco. "Strike Paralyzes San Francisco Life, But Unions Allow Entry of Food as Troops Help Police Keep Order" was the front-page headline in the *New York Times* on July 17, 1934.

The strike began when shipping companies refused to deal with the union the longshoremen had formed under Section 7 (a). Workers in other unions—truckers, cooks, fire fighters, pilots, engineers—supported the longshoremen by going on strike, too. On Thursday, July 5, 1934, fighting broke out between strikers and the police. Two men were killed, and seventy-three men were seriously injured. The day became known as Bloody Thursday. On Monday, fifteen thousand workers marched in memory of the dead workers. More workers went on strike. Picket lines stretched across the highways leading into San Francisco.

Roosevelt was on his way to Hawaii on board the U.S.S.

Houston. Cordell Hull, secretary of state, was the acting president. He and the attorney general, Homer Cummings, were very alarmed. Perkins was keeping her cool. "I had pretty good information on what was going on, not only from official but from private sources," she wrote later.

"I think federal troops should be sent in there to break this up," Hull told her.

Perkins protested against such drastic action.

"I don't think you see this in a serious enough light," Cummings said.

"I call it serious for us to use troops against American citizens who as yet haven't done anything except inconvenience the community...they haven't committed murder. They haven't rioted. They haven't interfered with the U.S. Mail, which was the excuse in the Pullman strike when [President] Cleveland used the army....I cannot tell you how serious it would be, politically, morally and for the basic labor-industry and labor-government relationships of the country, if we were to do this...," Perkins replied.

She insisted that they send a cable to Roosevelt asking for his authorization before they took any action. Then Perkins sent her own cable to Roosevelt.

Roosevelt supported Perkins's position. "Thanks for your estimate of situation," he replied in a cable. And he gave her authority to speak for him. "If you think advisable you can issue any statement or offer as coming from me or with my approval. It occurs to me the country as a whole may not understand the history of the strike and that with any statement you may want to clarify the issues publicly."

Perkins continued to calm things down, and within a week the strike was over. The longshoremen and shipowners agreed to settle their differences.

During her twelve years as secretary of labor, Perkins dealt

"Through the Mud Goes Madame Perkins" read the newspaper headline for the photograph of Perkins visiting shipyard workers in California. Henry Kaiser, the shipyard owner, is beside Perkins. (UPI/BETTMANN)

with many labor disputes. She received a lot of criticism from business leaders for not being tougher. But she never regretted her approach. According to Perkins,

> I have been called incompetent (and worse) because I have not prevented strikes and I am aware that there is a theory that if I were a two-fisted male I should be able to stop strikes. The accusation that I am a woman is incontrovertible. As for being two-fisted, I'm sure it is unrealistic and lacking in human knowledge to believe that getting tough or cracking down on working people would make things better. I believe that strikes and disputes should be settled on an equitable basis by negotiation, conciliation, and mu-

tual agreement. There have been two-fisted males in this office and strikes were never prevented, because no Secretary of Labor has ever had the authority or power directly to stop strikes, and it's doubtful if any clear thinking citizen would be willing to give to any agency of government the absolute right and power to interfere with other citizens.

CHAPTER EIGHT

Great Achievement

1934–1938

"It is a great satisfaction. . . ."

*I*n July 1934, shortly after the longshoremen's strike ended, Perkins created the Division of Labor Standards (DLS) to help "cooperate with the states in all problems of the health, safety, and working conditions of workers." It was the same year that Henry Ford, president of the Ford Motor Company, demonstrated his confidence in America's economic recovery by restoring the five-dollar-per-day minimum wage to most of the workers in his automobile factories. Continental Airlines was founded. *Mary Poppins,* a children's book by P. L. Travers, was published. So was *Murder on the Orient Express,* a mystery by Agatha Christie. A severe dust storm whooshed through states such as Texas, Oklahoma, and Kansas and blew three hundred million tons of topsoil all the way to the Atlantic Ocean.

Through the DLS, Perkins worked closely with state governments. "You are the first Secretary of Labor to show an interest in state departments of labor," the North Carolina commissioner of labor told Perkins. The DLS held programs to improve health conditions, regional conferences, and an annual national conference. It provided information about a wide variety of subjects, including workmen's compensation, and it offered a rigorous training course for factory inspectors. Concerned with occupational diseases, DLS investigated hazardous situations, including the Gauley Bridge disaster, where workers, mostly poor and black, were sent into work in a tunnel filled with dust containing 95 percent free silica, which could cause silicosis, a serious lung disease. The tunnel wasn't ventilated nor were the workers given face masks. When the men complained of shortness of breath, they were ignored.

Over a period of time, fifteen hundred men were disabled from silicosis and five hundred men died. The tragedy was covered over at first. But eventually a local newspaper uncovered it, and DLS investigated immediately. Without delay, Perkins organized a National Silicosis Conference to educate people about the health hazards and prevent a reoccurrence of such a tragedy.

Perkins was proud of the DLS. She felt that it had "probably done as much for the working people of the United States, by and large, as any one thing that we did." The DLS no longer exists today, but some of its mission is carried out by the Occupational Safety and Health Administration (OSHA).

Perkins spent a lot of time educating people about the need for social legislation and labor reform. Firmly believing that if people fully understood a situation they would do "the right thing," Perkins held press conferences, wrote articles, gave interviews, held meetings, and attended conventions. She traveled by train to give speeches in Philadelphia, Boston, Chicago, San Francisco, Atlanta, and other American cities. She also spoke on the radio. An exceptional speaker, Perkins had a unique ability to explain complicated issues in concrete terms—in human terms. In a poll of Washington broadcasters, Perkins was named among the five best political speakers in the country.

Her voice became very familiar to Americans, especially her Worcester accent which meant she said "laboh" for labor, "Frawnces" for Frances, and "cleah" for clear.

Unafraid to speak her mind, Perkins didn't hesitate to chide business leaders or labor leaders. According to a news account of a speech she gave in her hometown, Worcester, Massachusetts, she "took the Eastern section of the country to task for not understanding the problem of the farmer, she advocated the study of the farm situation by industrial and labor leaders." When she was testifying before Congress, she didn't hesitate to tell politicians to ask questions that made sense.

On one occasion during a meeting in her office, a group of business leaders refused to be introduced to William Green, a labor leader whom Perkins had invited. As the business leaders huddled in a corner, Perkins apologized to Green and he left. Then she turned to the business leaders. "I could not resist the

Perkins gave innumerable speeches. (N.Y. STATE SCHOOL OF INDUSTRIAL AND LABOR RELATIONS, CORNELL UNIVERSITY)

82

temptation to tell them that their behavior had surprised me and that I felt as though I had entertained eleven-year-old boys at their first party rather than men to whom the most important industry in the United States had been committed," Perkins later wrote.

Perkins's face became as familiar as her voice. She was pictured on the cover of *Time Magazine* and in numerous articles, including one in a very popular magazine, *Collier's,* with the headline "Fearless Frances."

In the summer of 1933, she threw herself into achieving two more of her goals—unemployment insurance and old-age insurance. She discussed the subjects at cabinet meetings, in hundreds of speeches to audiences in cities all over America, and in radio speeches. Of course, Perkins had been talking about these insurances for years. But now the American people were more inclined to listen. The Great Depression had shaken them awake to the perils of economic hard times when jobs were scarce.

Perkins stated in her popular book *People at Work,* which was published in 1934:

Perkins was often the subject of political cartoons. This one shows her holding scissors and approaching Samson, who represents labor unions. Uncle Sam, who represents national defense, is urging Perkins to cut Samson's hair, which would weaken him. (LIBRARY OF CONGRESS)

83

In a cartoon entitled "Gimme My Ships," Perkins is shown standing up to military and political leaders. (LIBRARY OF CONGRESS)

Americans who have learned so much out of these four years of depression often say with a great soberness that what we all need and want is a sense of security—the ability to make a plan that can look at least a year or two years ahead with some reliance that we can carry through that plan and that life will not be pulled out from under us by some inexplicable situation. In other words we are all tired of living in a cyclone area, and would like to live in a serene, sunny belt where peace of mind could have an opportunity to flower.

In the summer of 1934, Roosevelt finally appointed the Committee on Economic Security, a committee of cabinet members to develop a comprehensive social security program that included both unemployment and old-age insurance. He insisted that Perkins head the committee. "You care about this thing. You believe in it. Therefore I know you will put your back to it more than anyone else, and you will drive it through," Roosevelt told her.

And she did. For months, Perkins orchestrated a massive

effort to accumulate statistics, study plans in other countries, and answer such tough questions as how to pay for the social security system. A major concern was to propose a plan that would not be declared unconstitutional by the Supreme Court. According to Perkins, that problem seemed "almost insuperable" until she accidentally met Harlan Stone, a Supreme Court justice, at a party.

She told Justice Stone that she had "great hope of developing a social insurance system for our country." But, that she was uncertain how to finance it since the Supreme Court determined what was constitutional.

"The taxing power of the Federal Government, my dear; the taxing power is sufficient for everything you want and need," Stone whispered to Perkins.

"This was a windfall," Perkins later explained. "I told the President but bound him to secrecy as to the source of my sudden superior legal knowledge."

Roosevelt planned to present the proposal to Congress in January 1935. By November 1934, most of the plan was in place, with the exception of whether it would be run by the federal government alone or in cooperation with the states. Back and forth, committee members argued. Finally, the week before Christmas, Perkins "issued an ultimatum that the Committee would meet at eight o'clock at my house, all telephone service would be discontinued...and that we would sit all night, if necessary, until we had decided the thorny question once and for all. We sat until two in the morning, and at the end we agreed, reluctantly and with mental reservations, that for the present the wisest thing we could do was to recommend a federal-state system," Perkins wrote.

Roosevelt received the report and sent a request to Congress for social security legislation. On August 10, 1935, Congress finally approved the Social Security Act. In addition to old-age

Official portrait of Secretary of Labor Frances Perkins (U.S. DEPARTMENT OF LABOR)

insurance and unemployment insurance, the bill included programs to provide aid to people in need, such as blind people, people with disabilities, elderly poor people, and children under the age of eighteen in single-parent families (Aid to Dependent Children, or ADC).

Perkins knew that the act was not perfect; farm laborers and domestic workers weren't covered, and the committee had dropped health insurance after the American Medical Association had raised a ruckus. But she would fight for those another day. For now she savored the victory of achieving her lifelong goal of providing old-age and unemployment insurance to American workers.

"It is a great satisfaction to see the foundation stone laid in a security structure which aims to protect our people against the major hazards of life . . . ," Perkins told reporters. Today most Americans either do or will receive Social Security benefits. It is the most important and popular government program in America, a program that most Americans take for granted.

Roosevelt signed the Social Security Act on August 14 and Perkins arranged "a little ceremony." She invited members of Congress who had fought for the bill, and she had enough pens for Roosevelt to use as he signed the copies of the bill to give one to each person present. Except one for herself.

Roosevelt noticed. "Frances, where is your pen?" he asked.

"I haven't got one," she replied.

Turning to his secretary, Marvin McIntyre, Roosevelt said, "All right, give me a first class pen for Frances."

After official photographs were taken, Perkins took the train to New York City. Before the ceremony, Paul's nurse had called to tell her that he was missing. To avoid speculation by the press about her absence, Perkins went to the bill signing despite her concerns about Paul. Immediately afterward she left for New York where, with the help of friends, she found Paul unharmed.

While the Social Security Act met the Supreme Court's definition of constitutionality, the National Industrial Recovery Act did not. Two years after the NIRA was passed, the Supreme Court declared it unconstitutional.

Perkins was prepared.

She told Roosevelt, "I've got two bills which will do everything you and I think important under NRA. I have them locked up in the lower left-hand drawer of my desk against an emergency."

"There's New England caution for you, I declare," Roosevelt said with a laugh.

"But you and I agreed in February 1933 [their meeting when Perkins got Roosevelt's support for her list of programs] that putting a floor under wages and a ceiling over hours was essential. . . . We've explored the NRA . . . if it doesn't work or breaks down, we have to be prepared for something else," Perkins said.

Roosevelt told her to get the bills out of her drawer.

The first one established conditions under which goods and services purchased by the government were manufactured, including an eight-hour day, a forty-hour week, safety and health standards, a minimum wage, and prohibiting the use of children under the age of sixteen. It was introduced in the Senate by Senator Thomas Walsh and passed. Representative Arthur Healey introduced it in the House of Representatives. Known as the Walsh-Healey Public Contracts Act, it was passed in June 1936.

Perkins's second bill was broader. It covered all industries that engaged in interstate commerce, or that did business in more than one state (or produced goods that were used in more than one state). After many revisions, Perkins's bill became the Wages and Hours Act, or Fair Labor Standard Act. Finally passed in 1938, the bill abolished the employment of children under sixteen in interstate industry (eighteen in dangerous industries), established a minimum wage of forty cents an hour (in 1993, the minimum wage is $4.25), and a maximum work week of forty hours for all workers in interstate commerce. For work beyond forty hours a week, workers had to be paid "time and a half," or one and a half times the hourly wage.

When the bill finally passed, "Everybody claimed credit for it," Perkins wrote later. "I cannot remember whether the President and I claimed credit, but we always thought we had done it."

There was never any doubt that Perkins could claim full credit for getting the United States to join the International Labor Organization (ILO), an organization based in Geneva,

Switzerland, that was established to improve working conditions worldwide. In 1936 she attended an ILO conference in Geneva. It was the same year that Roosevelt was nominated to run for his second term as president. He won in a landslide. That was also the same year that Jesse Owens, an African-American athlete, won four gold medals in track and field at the summer Olympics in Berlin, causing Hitler to leave the stadium in rage. Civil war broke out in Spain, and the first Howard Johnson's Restaurant opened on Cape Cod, Massachusetts.

Perkins addressed the ILO conference, the first American cabinet member to ever speak at any official conference in Geneva. She was warmly received. According to one newspaper report; "If there were any vote in the International Labor Organization to decide who is the world's outstanding secretary of labor, it is a good guess that Miss Perkins now would win it. . . ."

On her way to Geneva, Perkins stopped in Paris, France, where she received an award as "the world's outstanding woman," from the Congress of International Federation of Business and Professional Women.

Back in America, however, not everyone was so enthusiastic.

CHAPTER NINE

Storms and Trials

1939–1940

"It hurt."

I haven't a flair for publicity. . . . I am not cozy and revealing with reporters. I can't say, 'Come in, boys,' and I wouldn't if I could because I don't think of them as 'boy,' " Perkins wrote in a magazine article. On another occasion she referred to her "lamentable lack of instinct for publicity." In addition to her poor public-relations skills, Perkins was an outspoken and independent woman. She had power and influence, and she did not use her husband's name, all of which was very radical in the 1930s. She also refused to knuckle under to pressure from politicians and business and labor leaders. She was not rude or hostile, just firm. And she was totally honest.

Increasingly, members of Congress criticized Perkins. So did the press. Stories started to appear with headlines such as "The Unpopular Mme. Perkins." Reporters wrote that she talked as if she "swallowed a press release" and that she was "too individualistic and militant. . . ."

Usually Perkins ignored the criticism. But a "whispering campaign" that she was really "a foreign-born Jew" named

Matilda Wutzki, who had married a Paul Wilson in February 1910, was too much. Perkins issued a letter in which she stated that she got married in 1913 and that there were no Jews in her background. But, Perkins wrote, "If I were a Jew I would make no secret of it. On the contrary, I would be proud to acknowledge it." In addition, Perkins wrote, "The utter un-Americanism of such a whispering campaign, the appeal to racial prejudice and the attempt at political propaganda by unworthy innuendo must be repugnant to all honorable men and women."

On March 12, 1938, Perkins's daughter, Susanna, got married. The wedding was held in New York City. Paul was well enough to attend and participate in the festivities. "Getting a daughter married takes one back to the beginnings of things, and old forgotten, half-completed affections, intentions, purposes, hopes and disappointments. The emotional upheaval that mothers go through on such an occasion is undoubtedly a helpful purge, but it is extremely difficult," Perkins wrote to a friend.

Even more emotionally hard times were about to hit.

In May 1938, the House of Representatives set up a committee to investigate un-American activities, which at that time meant being a communist. Martin Dies, a representative from Texas, was the chairman. By mid-August, Dies's committee had declared that at least 280 labor unions and 483 newspapers were communist. By the end of August, he branded Harry Bridges a communist. An alien who lived in San Francisco, Bridges was a longshoreman and labor leader. Dies said that Bridges was a communist and that he should be deported. Since the Bureau of Immigration was in the Department of Labor, Dies put pressure on Perkins to deport Bridges. Perkins refused without going through the proper legal steps.

During the time of the longshoremen's strike Perkins had met Bridges in San Francisco. "He was a small, thin, somewhat haggard man in a much-worn overcoat, the collar turned up and pinned around his throat, and with a cap in his hand. He was polite, deferential, hardly finding the voice to make demands for the striking longshoremen. His suggestions seemed practical and reasonable," Perkins later wrote.

Dies kept after Perkins. She investigated Bridges and discovered no evidence that he was a communist, only that he worked every day, paid his rent promptly, and spent most nights in his room playing his mandolin.

Still Dies kept after Perkins. Then on January 24, 1939, J. Parnell Thomas, a representative from New Jersey, introduced a forty-page resolution of impeachment against Perkins and two of her staff members. They were charged with "high crimes and misdemeanors in violation of the Constitution and the laws of the United States . . . for failing, neglecting, and refusing to enforce the immigration laws. . . ."

Perkins was stunned. The story was on the front page of newspapers across America. It was a terrible time for her. She tried to follow her grandmother's saying, "You do what is your duty to do and then act as if nothing had happened." She increased her church attendance to every day. "I find that I have great difficulty in praying for my enemies. It is very difficult. I grow confused," she told her pastor.

The resolution of impeachment was referred to the Committee on the Judiciary of the House. Perkins volunteered to appear before it. She sat at a small table in front of twenty-five members of the committee who sat behind a large, curved, raised table. In detail she discussed the Bridges case. Then she expressed her faith and confidence in the committee "to protect me and to secure my rights and reputation if I have done no wrong. . . ."

On March 24, 1939, the committee issued a report "that sufficient facts" were not presented to support the resolution of impeachment. The charges against Perkins and her staff members were dropped.

A few days later, Perkins said that she was grateful "that men of responsibility laid aside prejudices against me, against women, against partisan groups, and exercised their responsibility as Congressmen of the United States." All she ever said about how it felt to be impeached was that "it hurt." In 1948, J. Parnell Thomas was sentenced to six to eighteen months in prison for padding his congressional payrolls. His secretary, Helen Campbell, turned him in.

As it always had, Perkins's religious faith sustained her. Since 1933, she had gone at least once a month to an Episcopal convent in Catonsville, Maryland. It took her an hour to get there by train and taxi. She usually spent a day or a half a day there. The reverend mother and fourteen other nuns knew that she was the secretary of labor, but they did not tell anyone else. In official Washington, only her longtime secretary, Frances Jurkowitz, or Jay, knew where she went. Except for two hours a day, the nuns and visitor observed the rule of silence. No one talked.

Years later, Perkins wrote in a letter to a friend who was recovering from an operation for cancer of the throat and had to be silent, "I have discovered the rule of silence is one of the most beautiful things in the world. It gives one time for so many, many ideas and occupations. It also preserves one from the temptation of the idle word, the fresh remark, the wisecrack, the angry challenge, the hot-tempered reaction, the argument about nothing, the foolish question, the unnecessary noise of the human clack-clack. It is really quite remarkable what it does for one."

In 1940, Roosevelt ran for another term as president, the first man to be nominated three times. During the campaign, the Republican candidate, Wendell Wilkie, said during a speech that he would appoint a new secretary of labor. "And it won't be a woman either!" Wilkie added.

Roosevelt and Perkins heard Wilkie's speech on the radio.

"That was a boner Wilkie pulled. . . . Why did he have to insult every woman in the United States? It will make them mad, it will lose him votes," Roosevelt later told Perkins.

In November 1940, Roosevelt scored a big win over Wilkie. It was a tense time in the United States. Hitler's armies were on the march. Austria had fallen, as had Czechoslovakia, Poland, Norway, and Denmark. Roosevelt announced that the U.S. policy had changed from "neutrality" to "non-belligerency," which meant that America was not declaring war on Germany, yet, but it was openly supporting the Allies.

Frances Perkins had serious doubts about serving another term as secretary of labor. Of the original nine cabinet members, five remained. Of those five, two more would be replaced in 1940. But not Perkins. Roosevelt would not let her go.

She tried to convince him. She had achieved most of her goals. She had job offers that would ease her financial pressures. The newspapers were full of speculation and rumors. "Miss

Perkins greeting Roosevelt after his return from a trip to Teheran. "I am bound to him by ties of affection, common purpose, and joint undertakings," she once wrote. They also shared a strong sense of humor.
(FRANKLIN D. ROOSEVELT LIBRARY)

Perkins Quits Cabinet; Views Her Job as Finished" read one headline. Roosevelt's press secretary denied it. "If and when I get ready to announce my resignation, I will do it myself," Perkins said.

Privately, Perkins pressed Roosevelt to accept her resignation. He stalled her. Finally she talked to Eleanor Roosevelt and asked her to get an answer from Roosevelt.

Within a week, Perkins received a note from Eleanor Roosevelt, "I have talked to him about it, and the answer is no, absolutely no."

At the next cabinet meeting, Roosevelt asked Perkins, "Did you hear from my Mrs?"

"Yes, it's bright of you to communicate with me like that," Perkins replied.

"Well, I meant to tell you myself, but the more I thought of it, the more I didn't see how I was going to do it. . . . I know who you are, what you are, what you'll do, what you won't do. You know me. You see lots of things that most people don't see. You keep me guarded against a lot of things that no new man walking in here would protect me from," Roosevelt said.

Perkins could not refuse Roosevelt's personal appeal. So, just when America was about to plunge into another disaster, Perkins agreed to serve a third term as the secretary of labor.

CHAPTER TEN

War

1941–1945

"I felt I must stand by. . . ."

On December 7, 1941, hundreds of Japanese planes took off from carriers and headed toward Pearl Harbor, the major United States naval base in Hawaii. In a surprise attack, the Japanese pilots sank or disabled nineteen U.S. ships, including six battleships, destroyed 150 planes, and killed almost 2,500 soldiers, sailors, and civilians.

Perkins was in New York City. She later wrote that she was "locked up in a room in my club [the Cosmopolitan Club] with my secretary, writing an important report, and had seen no one and had heard no radio when the telephone call came from the White House to tell me to be at a cabinet meeting 'at eight o'clock tonight.'"

She asked the operator what was the matter.

"Just the war, what's in the papers," the operator replied, and hung up.

Perkins rushed to the airport. Two other cabinet members were there, too. Upon arriving in Washington, they went directly to the White House.

"The President nodded as we came in.... This was one of the few occasions he couldn't muster a smile..." Perkins wrote. "However he was calm, not agitated." Roosevelt told the cabinet members the story of the attack "briefly and simply." Then they left and Roosevelt called in leaders of Congress. Early the next morning, Perkins was in her office. "We will find the strength to meet this," she told her staff.

That day, December 8, the United States Congress declared war on Japan, and the United States entered World War II. Britain also declared war on Japan, and Japan declared war on the United States and Britain. On December 11, Germany and Italy declared war on the United States. Congress declared war on Germany and Italy.

Even before Pearl Harbor, the defense industry started to thrive in America as goods were sent to England and France and stockpiled in America. Jobs were plentiful. The number of strikes dramatically increased as workers felt secure enough to demand better conditions and more money. In an attempt to restore order, Perkins suggested the creation of a board of mediation for defense industries that could help settle disputes.

"I took pains to sell the idea to labor," Perkins wrote. That was no easy task. In 1938, a new national labor organization, the Congress of Industrial Organizations (CIO), split off from the AFL. Now Perkins had to deal with two competing national labor organizations. John L. Lewis was the president of the CIO. William Green headed the AFL. Perkins met with the leaders and convinced them to accept the idea of a board of mediation. They did, as long as they had equal representation. So on March 19, 1941, Roosevelt created a National Defense Mediation Board. It lasted until November, when John L. Lewis and the CIO delegates resigned because they did not get their way on a particular issue. The board ceased to function.

"The President asked me to think of something else. I

racked my brain and proposed that we hold a conference of labor and employer representatives and . . . try to get agreement on principles of labor relations . . . ," Perkins recalled.

On December 18, eleven days after Pearl Harbor, twelve leaders from industry and twelve labor leaders—six from the AFL and six from the CIO—gathered in Washington to attend Perkins's conference, the five-day War-Labor Conference. John L. Lewis was there. According to Perkins, he "was sobered by the reality and horror of the sudden war and all it meant to the country." So were the other labor and business leaders.

The conference "developed into one of the most interesting ever held in Washington," Perkins wrote later. Perkins met with individual participants and with groups of participants. She listened. She talked. She prodded. She encouraged labor and

Perkins and labor leaders leaving the White House after a meeting with Roosevelt. Facing the camera, from left to right, are: Philip Murray, Sidney Hillman, Matthew Woll, Perkins, Harry C. Bates, and John L. Lewis. (U.S. DEPARTMENT OF LABOR)

business leaders to express their frank opinions. "We . . . worked nights and argued and persuaded to the point of fatigue," Perkins later wrote.

Finally, the participants declared peace, at least for the duration of the war. There would be no strikes or lockouts, disputes would be settled by negotiation and collective bargaining, and all unsettled matters would be referred to a board that the president appointed, and the board's decision would be final.

On January 12, 1942, Roosevelt established the National War Labor Board. "One can say the War Labor Board was a success. . . . The pledges were kept, if imperfectly," Perkins later wrote.

Since the Japanese bombed Pearl Harbor, there were rumors that Japanese Americans were spies and saboteurs. Although there was absolutely no proof that Japanese Americans were a threat, some military officers pressured Roosevelt to do something. On February 20, 1942, Roosevelt issued Executive Order 9066 and authorized the "relocation" of Japanese Americans from their homes along the Pacific coast and in Arizona to concentration camps in Colorado, Utah, Arkansas, and other locations.

For years, Perkins had fought to protect the rights of all people, including aliens. She had abolished her predecessor's "secret squad." She had refused to be bullied into deporting Harry Bridges. At her impeachment hearing, she had said that "American institutions [must] operate without fear or favor and in the spirit of fair play to the stranger within our gates as well as to the native born."

However, Roosevelt did not consult her about Executive Order 9066, for in 1940, the Bureau of Immigration had been moved from the Department of Labor to the Department of Justice. For five years, Perkins herself had suggested that the bureau should be relocated because it really did not deal with labor issues. However, she thought it should be moved to the Department of the Interior and "be treated as one of the humanitarian functions of government." But because Roosevelt was worried about spies and saboteurs, he decided to move the bureau to the Department of Justice, where it was in charge of enforcing Executive Order 9066.

By September one hundred thousand Japanese Americans, two-thirds of them U.S. citizens, had been relocated into internment camps. Although Perkins never publically criticized Roosevelt's action, privately she thought that it was "very wrong." In 1988, Congress passed legislation apologizing for the internment and awarding restitution payment of twenty-thousand dollars each to the sixty thousand people still living who had been relocated to a camp.

World War II was an enormous tragedy. More than twenty million people died on the battlefields, in concentration camps, and in bombing raids on cities and towns, and thirty million were wounded. The financial cost was over a trillion dollars, plus property damage that was impossible to calculate.

Before the war, factory work was considered too dirty, too hard, and too dangerous for women to do. But as men left their jobs to fight the war, women were hired to build ships, planes, guns, trucks, and other supplies. In 1942, Perkins reported that at least four million American women were involved working in war industries. Millions more were working "in laboratories, banks, businesses, ticket offices, at automobile stations and airports, on buses, trucks, trolley cars, trains, as tax collectors, radio announcers, elevator operators, policemen, guards, messengers, and in numerous other occupations," Perkins said.

"A definitely encouraging trend has been a breakdown in many quarters of the prejudices against certain types of women workers," Perkins reported. Before the war, industries and government rarely hired women who were over thirty-five years old or married. Black women were usually only hired as domestic workers or farmhands. With the war, that changed. Older women, Perkins wrote, "are finding themselves at long last acceptable and employable." So were married women. And, "Negro women . . . are gaining footholds in a number of occupational fields formerly closed to them."

People with disabilities were also employed in larger numbers than ever before. "One of the items which most interested Roosevelt in reports on labor supply for the war industries was that blind, deaf, and semi-crippled [Roosevelt himself was "semi-crippled"] people were being given opportunity to work and were doing well," Perkins later wrote.

Perkins coined the term "Rosie the Riveter" to refer to women who worked in war industries. Like Uncle Sam, Rosie the Riveter became a national hero. Posters, magazine covers, and advertisements exhorting women to work in war industries showed Rosie as a white woman with a red bandanna with white polka dots wrapped around her short black hair, her right arm raised in a fist and her left hand pulling up her sleeve to show her muscle. Printed above her head were the words "We Can Do It!"

Perkins was determined that women would not be pushed out of the job market after the war. In a speech to the Women's Trade Union League, she said, "we must see to it that such women . . . are given their due chance. . . . Women must not be unfairly accused of taking men's jobs, as at the close of the last war [World War I]. When this war is over, government, labor, and industry, in making plans for our labor force, must not overlook the needs of American women who . . . have made their contributions and their sacrifices, too, for victory and democracy."

She was also determined to maintain the gains she had fought so hard to win for better wages, hours, working conditions, and the abolition of child labor. It was no easy task. Employers claimed that the laws slowed down production. Eager to show their patriotism, some politicians proposed legislation to repeal all or part of state and federal labor laws. But Perkins marshalled her facts and statistics and pointed out that safe working conditions reduced costly industrial accidents. She convinced Roosevelt, and they agreed that labor laws should only be suspended temporarily and with provisions to safeguard the basic needs of the workers.

Roosevelt announced that, "We must accept the principle which has been established for years, that the eight-hour day is the most efficient productive day for the worker. . . . Protection of workers against accidents, illness, and fatigue are vital for efficiency."

"The result of his stand was that we were able eventually to stem the tide of repeal of labor legislation. . . . We came through the war with basic labor legislation intact," Perkins wrote later.

In 1944, Roosevelt decided to run for a fourth term as President. The end of the war was in sight. On June 6, the United States and Great Britain launched D Day Operation Overlord and invaded German-occupied France. In September, the U.S. Army entered Germany for the first time. In October, the U.S. Navy inflicted a major defeat on the Imperial Japanese Navy in the Battle of Leyte Gulf. Nineteen forty-four was also the year numbers of Americans continued to move from rural areas to cities. *Seventeen,* a magazine for girls, first appeared in the United States. And in Amsterdam, the Netherlands, Anne Frank, a young Jewish girl, and her family, who had been hiding from the German Gestapo, were betrayed. Anne Frank died a year later in a concentration camp. Three notebooks in which she wrote while she was hiding with her family were later found, and their contents published as *The Diary of a Young Girl.*

In November, Roosevelt was reelected. Again Frances Perkins tried to resign. This time she wrote a long letter. In it she detailed her accomplishments. "With one major exception all the items we discussed as 'among the practical possibilities' before you took office as President [for the first time in 1933] have been accomplished or begun. The exception is a social security item providing for some form of benefit to persons where loss of income is due to sickness and provision for appropriate medical care for the same. I hope that this will be upon your agenda for the near future." Medicare, or health insurance for people with severe disabilities or for people over the age of sixty-five years old, was added to Social Security by Congress in 1965.

Although Roosevelt kept putting her off, Perkins was determined. "I packed my books and papers. Carpets were cleaned and chairs reupholstered. Everything was in readiness for a successor," Perkins later wrote. She also informed her colleagues at the Department of Labor.

Finally, Roosevelt agreed to accept her resignation. He told her that he would make the announcement on inauguration day, January 20, 1945. Perkins went to what she thought would be her last cabinet meeting. She even wrote Roosevelt a note reminding him to tell the other cabinet members it was her last meeting. Perkins assumed that Roosevelt would make a "nice little speech . . . all the amenities would be observed and we would part in friendly fashion."

But, Roosevelt did not say anything. So, after the meeting, Perkins asked to talk with him.

"As I sat down beside him I had a sense of his enormous fatigue. He had the pallor, the deep gray color, of a man who had been long ill. . . . In a hospital a nurse would have put her arm behind him and lowered him down onto his pillow. . . . His lips were blue. His hand shook. I hated to press him, but I had to," Perkins wrote later.

Perkins suggested that he get his press secretary to announce her resignation.

"No," Roosevelt said, "Frances, you can't go now. You mustn't put this on me now. I just can't be bothered now. I can't think of anybody else, and I can't get used to anybody else. Not now! Do stay there and don't say anything. You are all right. . . . Frances, you have done awfully well. I know what you have been through. I know what you have accomplished. Thank you."

Roosevelt gripped Perkins's hand. Tears filled his eyes. And hers.

"It was all the reward that I could ever have asked—to know that he had recognized the storms and trials I had faced in developing our program, to know that he appreciated the program and thought well of it, and that he was grateful.

"I could not say more, although I felt, intellectually and logically, that I ought to have insisted that the resignation go through. I could not insist. I felt I must stand by until this pressure and strain were over," Perkins wrote later.

On inauguration day, Roosevelt officially responded to the letter of resignation Perkins had sent him earlier. In the last paragraph, he wrote, "There are many other things to do— matters with which you are familiar—and, as I told you on Friday [the day of what she thought was her last cabinet meeting], your resignation is not one of them. It is hereby declined. Indeed, it is rejected and refused."

In February, Roosevelt went to Yalta, a resort on the Black Sea, to meet with Winston Churchill, the leader of Great Britain, and Joseph Stalin, the leader of the Soviet Union. Together the men made plans, most of which were kept secret, about how to deal with Germany and other matters after the war ended. Roosevelt returned looking much better.

In March, Roosevelt planned to go to Warm Springs, Georgia, a health resort. Perkins met with him the day before he left. Confidentially, Roosevelt told her that he and his wife, Eleanor, were going to England in May.

Since the war was still being fought, Perkins expressed concern about their safety.

"Although we were alone in the room, he put his hand to the side of his mouth and whispered, 'The war in Europe will be over by the end of May.'"

On April 12, 1945, Franklin Delano Roosevelt had a massive cerebral hemorrhage and died in Warm Springs, Georgia. Vice President Harry S. Truman became president.

On May 7, 1945, Germany formally surrendered. Japan formally surrendered on September 2, 1945.

In between that time, on May 23, 1945, Truman accepted Frances Perkins's resignation, effective on June 30, 1945.

At a testimonial dinner held in her honor, a host of labor, government, and industry leaders spoke in her honor. Although Molly Dewson was not able to attend, she helped plan the dinner. "I am so glad they gave Frances a good send off. How I should have enjoyed being there to see all the old gang," she wrote to a friend.

Perkins's old friend Robert Wagner, who had headed the Factory Investigating Committee years ago and was now a U.S. senator, spoke. "Frances Perkins was, and still is, the supreme student of social conditions and remedial social legislation. She uncovered the facts and told us what to do about them," Wagner said.

And, by doing so, Perkins achieved her goals. She was sixty-five years old, the age when most people retire. But there was still more for Frances Perkins to do.

CHAPTER ELEVEN

So Much More to Do

1946–1965

". . . the time has gone so fast."

On her last day as secretary of labor, Frances Perkins wore a jaunty black sailor hat. "I'm going into private life and this is my private hat," Perkins explained. But that did not mean she planned to retire.

In the fall, Perkins went to Paris to represent the United States at the annual meeting of the International Labor Organization in Paris. A book agent pursued her. He wanted her to write a biography of Franklin Roosevelt. Perkins had already refused several times. On her way to Paris, she stopped in London. The agent showed up with a contract. Again Perkins refused. Susanna, who was with her, talked her into saying yes. "Oh, do it, Mother. Don't be so stupid. Just do it!"

The book she wrote, *The Roosevelt I Knew,* was very successful. It is still considered one of the best biographies of Roosevelt. "I was exhausted at the end of it," Perkins said. But not too exhausted to accept Truman's appointment as a member of the three-member Civil Service Commission (CSC), the personnel agency in charge of government workers.

For six and a half years, Perkins prodded the government

to be more efficient, to cut down on red tape and to simplify rules and regulations. "I sometimes think that we are all like the file clerk who made himself indispensable by filing everything in the wrong place and then finding it. We make our rules so complex that they must be interpreted by experts," she said in one speech. In another she criticized government jargon, "You're not told to get ready, you're either activated or alerted," Perkins said. She also pointed out the inaccuracy of using "underprivileged" instead of "poor" in describing people without money: "I don't believe that's the correct word—at least they have the privilege of not having to keep up with the Joneses."

In 1952, Perkins attended her fiftieth reunion at Mount Holyoke. Sixty of her classmates were there, too. As permanent class president, Perkins presided over their festivities. It was a happy time. "I am deeply grateful for the love my classmates show me and for the strength that love gives me," Perkins later wrote to a classmate.

Seven months later, her husband died. The year before he had come to live with her in Washington. Throughout their marriage, Perkins provided for Paul and was always concerned about his well-being. He was buried in the Perkinses' family cemetery, just down the road from the Brick House, in Newcastle, Maine.

That same year, Dwight Eisenhower was elected president, the first Republican in twenty years. On his inauguration day, Perkins submitted her letter of resignation from the Civil Service Commission. At the age of seventy-two, Frances Perkins was leaving public office. On her last day, she commented to a reporter, "I was lucky to live at a time when the United States was ready for social reform. And I was lucky to live in a period when women finally got a chance to serve in public life."

Frances Perkins started a new career as a public speaker. A popular lecturer, she taught university seminars and spoke at conferences. After being honored at a women's rally in Albany, New York, Perkins wrote to her old friend Molly Dewson that the younger women were grateful for the older women's pioneering efforts. "It was something too, wasn't it! I sometimes pinch myself at realizing how far we came in making America Modern in the years 1910–1940," Perkins wrote.

In 1955, Perkins was hired as a visiting professor at the School of Labor and Industrial Relations at Cornell University in Ithaca, New York. Most of the students had not even been born when Perkins was appointed secretary of labor. For them, she was a living history book. Always a great storyteller with a flair for mimicry, Perkins delighted in telling students how things that they took for granted, such as Social Security, came into being.

She was greatly honored when the members of the Telluride Association, all men on academic scholarships at Cornell, invited her to live at their house as a guest-in-residence. No woman had ever been asked before, and so Perkins achieved another first. She was eighty years old. She had a wonderful time, as did the men of Telluride House. Perkins brought their flower garden back to life, shared Maine lobster dinners with them, and regaled them with stories from her extraordinary life.

Although few people knew it, Perkins's eyesight was failing. She was also growing shorter with age. "Be not afraid. It is I," Perkins once called out to an audience after she stepped up to a lectern that was taller than she was.

But her memory was as sharp as ever. On March 25, 1961, she commemorated an event that, fifty years earlier, had shaped her life—the Triangle Shirtwaist Company fire. Together with Eleanor Roosevelt, Rose Schneiderman, and twelve elderly survivors of the fire, Perkins attended a memorial service held at the corner of Washington Place and Greene Street, across the street from New York University. A plaque was placed on the building with the words: "Out of their martyrdom came new concepts of social responsibility and labor legislation that have helped make American working conditions the finest in the world."

Perkins celebrated another fifty-year celebration in 1963 when she spoke at a dinner commemorating the creation of the Department of Labor. President John F. Kennedy attended. Born in 1917, the year Perkins was thirty-seven years old, Kennedy was captivated by Perkins's stories. After reviewing her achievements, Kennedy reminded the audience that Perkins, "who looked so quiet and peaceful and sweet, was also one of the most controversial, dangerous figures that roamed the United States in the 1930s."

But now it was the 1960s, and people no longer questioned Perkins's controversial ideas. On the contrary, they took them

Perkins and President John F. Kennedy at the Fiftieth Anniversary Dinner of the founding of the Department of Labor (NATIONAL WOMEN'S HALL OF FAME)

for granted as they cashed their paychecks and counted on Social Security. "I endured a lot while I was in office, didn't I? But people are very ready to notice what you did when you are no longer a hazard to them. Funny but very nice!" Perkins once wrote in a letter to an old friend and colleague, Clara Beyer, who had helped her establish the Bureau of Labor Standards.

On May 14, 1965, Frances Perkins died in a New York City hospital. At the age of eighty-five, she had suffered a stroke and never regained consciousness.

Several years before her death, Perkins had talked about the state of the world. "I hear people say that the world is in a crisis. . . . I think crisis has occurred in the world's history many times, I'm glad to say that in those other crises we didn't have radio, television, and the movies to run it up until everybody died of terror. . . . You can't do any of the things we did in the early part of the century if you're afraid. . . . You just can't be afraid . . . if you're going to accomplish anything."

Clearly, Frances Perkins, a woman who achieved so much, was not afraid. Her faith, her commitment to social justice, her determination to do what was right kept her brave. So did her spunk and sense of humor.

Hundreds of people gathered to honor Frances Perkins at a funeral service in New York City. Another service was held at Cornell University. She was buried, in between the graves of her parents and husband, in the Perkinses' family cemetery in Newcastle, Maine, just down the road from the Brick House.

Frances Perkins's name and the dates of her birth and death are carved on her headstone. So are the words:

Secretary of Labor of U.S.A.
1933–1945

Frances Perkins's
headstone (PHOTOGRAPH
BY PENNY COLMAN)

Afterword

Sadly, Frances Perkins was right that the door might not open to other women for a "long, long time." Twenty years passed before another president, Dwight Eisenhower, appointed another woman, Oveta Culp Hobby, to the cabinet as secretary of health, education and welfare, a newly created cabinet position. Hobby served for two years. Forty-two years passed before President Gerald Ford appointed Carla Hills as secretary of housing and urban development, a cabinet position that had been created in 1965. Hills also served two years. Sixty years later President Bill Clinton appointed three women and eleven men to his cabinet.

Perkins was also right in knowing that the fight to maintain labor standards would be ongoing. As recently as 1991, twenty-five workers died in a factory fire in Raleigh, North Carolina. They were trapped behind locked doors and blocked fire escapes. After the fire, state officials admitted that the factory had never received a safety inspection. "There are probably too many places like this that we haven't even heard existed, nor have we inspected, that are in need of regular inspection," said North Carolina Labor Commissioner John Brooks.

That wouldn't surprise Frances Perkins. Nor would she be surprised to know that unemployment and health care are still problems. Perkins knew that her work was not done. But she trusted that there would be another generation of people who believed in social justice and who would fight to make life better for all Americans.

Chronology

1880*   Fannie Coralie Perkins born on April 10, in Boston, Massachusetts.

1882   Perkins family moved to Worcester, Massachusetts.

1898   Perkins graduated from Worcester Classical High School.

1902   Perkins graduated from Mount Holyoke College.

1904   Perkins started teaching in Lake Forest, Illinois.

1907   In the fall, Perkins moved to Philadelphia, Pennsylvania. She was the general secretary of the Philadelphia Research and Protective Association.

1909   Offered a fellowship to study in New York City, Perkins accepted and moved there.

1910   Perkins earned a master's degree from Columbia University. She was hired by the New York Consumers' League.

*Eighteen eighty-two is sometimes given as Perkins's birth date. She herself used that date on a Mount Holyoke alumnae form as early as 1923 and continued to use it. However, the date on her official birth certificate is 1880.

1911   On March 25, Frances Perkins witnessed the Triangle
       Shirtwaist Company fire, in which 146 workers
       died. In response, two major committees were or-
       ganized: the Committee on Public Safety and the
       Factory Investigating Commission. Perkins served
       as an expert witness and primary investigator.

1913   On September 26, Perkins married Paul Wilson.

1916   On December 30, Perkins's daughter, Susanna, was
       born.

1919   Governor Al Smith appointed Perkins a commissioner
       on the New York State Industrial Commission.

1921   Perkins served as executive secretary of the Council
       on Immigrant Education.

1922   Governor Smith was reelected and appointed Perkins
       a commissioner on the New York State Industrial
       Board.

1926   Smith appointed Perkins as chair of the New York
       State Industrial Board.

1929   Governor Franklin Roosevelt appointed Frances Per-
       kins as the New York State Industrial Commis-
       sioner. As commissioner, she became the first
       woman cabinet member in New York.

1933   President Franklin Roosevelt appointed Frances Per-
       kins as the U.S. secretary of labor, the first woman
       U.S. cabinet member.

1935   Perkins directed the development and passage of the
       Social Security Act.

1939   Perkins successfully defended herself against an im-
       peachment resolution.

1945   Roosevelt died. Perkins resigned as secretary of labor.

1946   Perkins wrote her very successful book, *The Roosevelt
       I Knew*. President Harry S. Truman appointed Per-
       kins to the U.S. Civil Service Commission.

1955   At the age of 75, Perkins became a visiting professor at Cornell University's School of Industrial and Labor Relations.

1965   On May 14, Frances Perkins died.

1980   Dedication of the U.S. Department of Labor headquarters in Washington, D. C., as the Frances Perkins Building.

1982   Frances Perkins inducted into the National Women's Hall of Fame.

1988   Frances Perkins inducted into the Labor Hall of Fame.

Cabinet Members Appointed
by President Franklin Delano Roosevelt

Department of State, 1789*

Cordell Hull   1933**
E. R. Stettinius, Jr   1944

Treasury Department, 1789

William H. Woodin   1933
Henry Morgenthau   1934

War Department, 1789
(In 1947, this became part of the Defense Department.)

George H. Dern   1933
Harry H. Woodring   1937
Henry L. Stimson   1940

*The date indicates the year that Congress created the department.
**The date indicates the year Roosevelt appointed the person as secretary of that department.

Office of Attorneys General, 1789
(In 1870, this office became the Department of Justice.)

Homer S. Cummings   1933
Frank Murphy   1939
Robert H. Jackson   1940
Francis Biddle   1941

Navy Department, 1798
(In 1947, this became part of the Defense Department.)

Claude A. Swanson   1933
Charles Edison   1940
Frank Knox   1940
James V. Forrestal   1944

Department of the Interior, 1849

Harold L. Ickes   1933

Department of Agriculture, 1889

Henry A. Wallace   1933
Claude R. Wickard   1940

Department of Commerce, 1903

Daniel C. Roper   1933
Harry L. Hopkins   1939
Jesse Jones   1940
Henry A. Wallace   1945

Department of Labor, 1913

Frances Perkins   1933

Places to Visit

Hull House, 800 S. Halsted Street, Chicago, Illinois.
Open: Monday to Friday, 10:00 A.M. to 4:00 P.M., and also on
   Sunday, noon to 5:00 P.M., in the summer. For information
   call 312-413-5353.

Labor Hall of Fame, Frances Perkins Building, Department of
   Labor, 200 Constitution Avenue, N.W., Washington, D.C.
Exhibit Hours: Monday to Friday, 8:15 A.M. to 4:45 P.M. For
   information call 202-371-6422.

Frances Perkins Plaque, Frances Perkins Building, Department
   of Labor, 200 Constitution Avenue, N.W., Washington, D.C.
Exhibit Hours: Monday to Friday, 8:15 A.M. to 4:45 P.M.
For information call 202-219-7316.

The National Women's Hall of Fame, 76 Fall Street, Seneca
   Falls, New York.
Exhibit hours: May to October: Monday to Saturday, 9:30 A.M.
   to 5:00 P.M.; Sunday, noon to 4:00 P.M. November to April:
   Wednesday to Saturday, 10:00 A.M. to 4:00 P.M.; Sunday, noon
   to 4:00 P.M.
For information call 315-568-2936.

Triangle Shirtwaist Company Fire Plaque, corner of Washington Place and Greene Street (campus of New York University), New York, New York.

Notes

All the quotations by Frances Perkins and others are taken from her extensive Oral History, her book *The Roosevelt I Knew,* or her class letters, which were published in the *Mount Holyoke Alumnae Quarterly.*

Information about Perkins's efforts on behalf of black workers in chapter six is drawn from an article, "Frances Perkins' Interest in a New Deal for Blacks" by Henry P. Guzda.

Information about CCC camps for unemployed women in chapter seven is drawn from *Beyond Suffrage: Women in the New Deal* by Susan Ware, pp. 111–114.

Information about the Division of Labor Standards in chapter eight is drawn from an article, "The Division of Labor Standards: Laying the Groundwork for OSHA," by Judson Edward MacLaury.

Bibliography

Bernstein, Irving. *Turbulent Years: A History of the American Worker, 1933–1941.* Boston: Houghton Mifflin, 1970.

Freidel, Frank. *Franklin D. Roosevelt: Launching the New Deal.* Boston: Little, Brown, 1973.

Goldmark, Josephine. *Impatient Crusader: Florence Kelley's Life Story.* Urbana: University of Illinois Press, 1953.

Hofstadter, Richard. *The Age of Reform: From Bryan to F.D.R.* New York: Alfred A. Knopf, 1955.

Ickes, Harold. *The Secret Diary of Harold L. Ickes.* 3 vols. New York: Simon and Schuster, 1953–1957.

Josephson, Matthew, and Hannah Josephson. *Al Smith: Hero of the Cities: A Political Portrait Drawing on the Papers of Frances Perkins.* Boston: Houghton Mifflin, 1969.

Lawson, Don. *Frances Perkins: First Lady of the Cabinet.* New York: Abelard-Schuman, 1966.

Learned, Henry Barrett. *The President's Cabinet.* New Haven: Yale University Press, 1912.

Leuchtenburg, William E. *Franklin D. Roosevelt and the New Deal: 1932–1940.* New York: Harper and Row, 1963

Martin, George. *Madam Secretary Frances Perkins: A Biography of America's First Woman Cabinet Member.* Boston: Houghton Mifflin, 1976.

Minutes of the New York State Factory Investigating Commission, New York Preliminary Report, vol. 2. Transmitted to the Legislature March 1, 1912. Albany: Argus, 1912.

Mohr, Lillian. *Frances Perkins, "That Woman in FDR's Cabinet."* Croton-on-Hudson, N.Y.: North River Press, 1979.

Morgan, Ted. *FDR: A Biography.* New York: Simon and Schuster, 1985.

Myers, Elisabeth. *Frances Perkins.* New York: Messner, 1979. (juvenile historic fiction)

Perkins, Frances. *People at Work.* New York: John Day, 1934.

————. *The Roosevelt I Knew.* New York: Viking Press, 1946.

Riis, Jacob A. *The Children of the Poor.* New York: Charles Scribner's Sons, 1898.

Roosevelt, Eleanor. *This I Remember.* New York: Harper and Brothers, 1949.

Roosevelt, Eleanor, and Lorena A. Hickok. *Ladies of Courage.* New York: G. P. Putnam's Sons, 1954.

Severn, Bill. *Frances Perkins: A Member of the Cabinet.* New York: Hawthorn Books, 1976. (young adult)

Sicherman, Barbara, and Carol Hurd Green, eds. *Notable American Women: The Modern Period.* Cambridge: Harvard University Press, Belknap Press, 1980.

Sims, Carolyn. *Labor Unions in the United States.* New York: Franklin Watts, 1971.

Sitkoff, Harvard. *New Deal for Blacks: The Emergence of Civil Rights as a National Issue.* Vol 1: *The Depression Decade.* New York: Oxford University Press, 1978.

Stein, Leon. *The Triangle Fire.* Philadelphia: J. B. Lippincott, 1962.

Tinker, Irene. *Women in Washington.* Beverly Hills: Sage Publications, 1983.

Ware, Susan. *Beyond Suffrage: Women in the New Deal.* Cambridge: Harvard University Press, 1981.

Wehle, Louis B. *Hidden Threads of History.* New York: Macmillan, 1953.

Wertheimer, Barbara Mayer. *We Were There: The Story of Working Women in America.* New York: Pantheon Books, 1977.

SELECTED ARTICLES BY FRANCES PERKINS

"Some Facts Concerning Certain Undernourished Children." *Survey* 25 (October 1, 1910): 68–72.

"The Fire Bills." *Survey* 29 (February 22, 1913): 732–733.

"My Job." *Survey* 61 (March 15, 1929): 773–775.

"Helping Industry to Help Itself." *Harper's* 161 (October 1930): 624–630.

"Social Security: the Foundation." *New York Times Magazine,* August 18, 1935. 1–2, 15.

"Eight Years as Madame Secretary." *Fortune* 24 (Sept. 1941): 76–79, 94.

"Women's Work in Wartime." *Monthly Labor Review,* U.S. Bureau of Labor Statistics, Washington, D.C. April 1943.

SELECTED ARTICLES ABOUT FRANCES PERKINS AND RELATED ISSUES

Adams, Mildred. "To the Woman in Politics Comes Also a New Deal." *New York Times Magazine,* April 30, 1933: 4, 16.

Guzda, Henry P. "Frances Perkins' Interest in a New Deal for Blacks." *Monthly Labor Review,* April 1980: 31–35.

Hinshaw, Augusta W. "The Story of Frances Perkins." *Century* 114 (September 1927): 596–605.

Lord, Russell. "Madame Secretary: A Profile." *New Yorker,* September 2 and 9, 1933.

MacLaury, Judson Edward. "The Division of Labor Standards: Laying the Groundwork for OSHA." *Applied Industrial Hygiene,* December 1988: F-8– F-11.

Parkhurst, Genevieve. "Is Feminism Dead?" *Harper's* 170 (May 1935): 735–745.

"Truce at a Crisis." *Time,* August 14, 1933. (Frances Perkins is on the cover.)

Tucker, Ray. "Fearless Frances." *Collier's* 94 (July 28, 1934): 16, 35.

Woolf, S. J. "Miss Perkins Sees New Hope for Labor." *New York Times Magazine,* August 5, 1934: 3, 10.

For a brief overview of the lives of Frances Perkins, Mary "Molly" Dewson, Mary Dreier, Eleanor Roosevelt, and Rose Schneiderman, see: *Notable American Women: The Modern Period.* Cambridge: Harvard University Press, 1980.

For a brief overview of the life of Florence Kelley, see: *Notable American Women: A Biographical Dictionary,* vol 2. Cambridge: Harvard University Press, 1971.

Documentary Film

Potts, Marjory, and Robert Potts. "You May Call Her Madam Secretary." (16 mm film or videocassette) West Tisbury, Mass.: Vineyard Video Productions, 1986.

Poster

A poster of Frances Perkins is distributed by the Organization for Equal Opportunity of the Sexes, P.O. Box 438, Blue Hill, Minnesota 04614.

Index

Made in the USA
Coppell, TX
27 July 2020